Tim Lautzenheiser

A Teaching Music through
Performance in Band
20th Anniversary Edition

Also available from GIA Publications

Teaching Music through Performance in Band
Volume 1 (Second Edition) • G-4484
Resource Recordings:
Grades 2-3 • CD-418   Grade 4 • CD-490
Grade 5 • CD-817   Grade 6 • CD-818

Volume 2 • G-4889
Resource Recordings:
Grades 2-3 • CD-446   Grades 4-5 • CD-551

Volume 3 • G-5333
Resource Recordings:
Grades 2-3 • CD-473   Grade 4 • CD-510

Volume 4 • G-6022
Resource Recordings:
Grades 2-3 • CD-552   Grades 4-5 • CD-603

Volume 5 • G-6573
Resource Recordings:
Grades 2-3 • CD-623   Grades 4-5 • CD-638

Volume 6 • G-7027
Resource Recordings:
Grades 2-3 • CD-683   Grades 4-5 • CD-684

Volume 7 • G-7436
Resource Recordings:
Grades 2-3 • CD-780   Grades 4-5 • CD-816

Volume 8 • G-7926
Resource Recordings:
Grades 2-3 • CD-849   Grade 4 • CD-876

Volume 9 • G-8433
Resource Recordings:
Grades 2-3 • CD-899   Grades 4-5 • CD-945

Volume 10 • G-8876
Resource Recordings:
Grades 2-3 • CD-960   Grades 4-5 • CD-980

Teaching Music through Performance in Band
Solos with Wind Band Accompaniment • G-8188

**Teaching Music through Performance
in Middle School Band**
Volume 1 • G-8871
Resource Recording • CD-963

Teaching Music through Performance in Jazz
Volume 1 • G-7268
Resource Recording • CD-772

Volume 2 • G-9031
Resource Recording • CD-1001

**Teaching Music through Performance in Jazz
for Beginning Ensembles**
Volume 1 • G-9022
Resource Recording • CD-1000

**Teaching Music through Performance
in Beginning Band**
Volume 1 • G-5337
Resource Recording • CD-485

Volume 2 • G-7264
Resource Recording • CD-750

**Teaching Music through Performing
Marches • G-5684**
Resource Recording • CD-563

Teaching Music through Performance in Orchestra
Volume 1 • G-5565
Resource Recording: Grades 1-3 • CD-536

Volume 2 • G-6091
Resource Recording: Grades 1-3 • CD-615

Volume 3 • G-7191
Resource Recording: Grades 1-4 • CD-751

Teaching Music through Performance in Choir
Volume 1 • G-6534
Resource Recording: Levels 1-4 • CD-650

Volume 2 • G-7100
Resource Recording: Levels 1-5 • CD-719

Volume 3 • G-7522
Resource Recording: Levels 1-5 • CD-869

**Teaching Music through Performance
in Middle School Choir**
Volume 1 • G-7397
Resource Recordings:
Set 1 • CD-854   Set 2 • CD-927

Tim Lautzenheiser

A Teaching Music through Performance in Band 20th Anniversary Edition

GIA Publications, Inc.

Chicago

For a complete, searchable index of works covered in the Teaching Music Series, as well as audio clips of more than 1000 pieces, visit the website TeachingMusic.org.

A Teaching Music through Performance in Band
20th Anniversary Edition
Tim Lautzenheiser

www.teachingmusic.org

Layout: Martha Chlipala

GIA Publications, Inc.
7404 S Mason Ave
Chicago IL 60638
www.giamusic.com

G-9342
ISBN: 978-1-57999-220-9

Table of Contents

Let the Music Begin

Tim Lautzenheiser

It was during Midwest Clinic (circa early 1990s) when six people crammed into one small hotel room at the Hilton in downtown Chicago. Richard Miles, Morehead State University Director of Bands, proposed the idea of writing a book that contained front chapters written by each member of the invited team followed by Teacher Resource Guides that analyzed 100 of the best-known foundational band compositions. The idea was presented to Alec Harris at GIA Publications, and with an affirmative response, everyone went to work on this exciting project.

Little did we know that *Teaching Music through Performance in Band* was destined to become an ever-growing, multi-volume succession of landmark texts embracing a wide span of the music education curriculum. Thanks to the steadfast commitment of Richard Miles and the immeasurable support of Alec Harris, the Teaching Music series continues as a mainstay in personal and professional libraries of music conductors, directors, and educators around the world. From all indications, there will be many more editions yet to come in the future; it truly is an endless landscape of possibilities.

For the record book, the cast of original six authors still meets every December at Midwest Clinic. The good news is that we have found a bigger room at the hotel so everyone now has a place to sit!

If I Knew Then What I Know Now...

We all have said, "If I had it to do over…," and followed that with a litany of what we would do differently if we could somehow jump in the illusive time machine and REDO, RELIVE, and REINVENT some aspects of our professional pathways. It seems like a pointless exercise, but perhaps not.

My hope is that some young educator will read this chapter and one of my following Top 10 "If I Knew Then What I Know Now" mantras will resonate and offer some positive road signs for his/her successful future.

#1
I would be more judicious about the use of time.

Time is the one commodity we cannot bank. We can't save it…we either spend it or lose it. It is the one factor that "evens the game board of life." We all have 24 hours a day. The burning introspective question is: Do we spend it devoting ourselves to our art, our mission, our passion, our contribution to this world so our lives MAKE A POSITIVE DIFFERENCE?

> "Success has nothing to do with what you gain in life; it's measured by what you do for others."
>
> —Danny Thomas

#2
I would be more accepting of "what is."

Being frustrated or upset by "what is" demonstrates our unwillingness to accept what life brings our way. "Happiness is not getting what we want; happiness is wanting what we get."

It's always interesting when people say, "That shouldn't have happened!" Well, in truth, it must have "should have happened" because it *did* happen. Rather than waste time, effort, and energy being at odds with this realization, it would be more advantageous to accept "what is" and move forward accordingly.

> "The pessimist sees the challenge in every opportunity; the optimist sees the opportunity in every challenge."
>
> —Winston Churchill

#3
I would be more conscious of my attitude and how it impacts others; moreover, I would realize that I have control over it.

At every moment, we are either appreciating or depreciating our environment; there is no neutral stance. Knowing this, we always have the opportunity to make things better, contribute more, share with others, advance the cause by presenting a positive attitude to all within our reach. We can *always* upgrade our attitude and see every situation in a more worthy light.

> "When we change the way we look at things, the things we look at change."
> —Wayne Dyer

#4
I would be more proactive and less reactive.

If we take the time to "choose to understand before being understood" (thank you, Stephen Covey), we could gain so much. The master teachers have the talent to "get behind the eyes of others." Before jumping to conclusions, they always look for the answer that will bring consensus and calm to the environment. While it is certainly not 100% true, *proactive* tends to be POSITIVE and *reactive* tends to be NEGATIVE.

> "The proactive approach to a mistake is to acknowledge it instantly, correct and learn from it."
> —Stephen Covey

#5
I would get out of my comfort zone and take advantage of every opportunity for all it is worth.

Instead of always "playing it safe," choosing the pathway of least resistance, avoiding the opportunity to breakthrough self-doubt, we know that the best learning, growing, becoming is always the result of pushing oneself beyond the known comfort zone—embracing new challenges, not being held back by fear, but tapping into the endless imagination of taking action by asking, "What if?"

"The garden of the world has no limits, except in your mind."
—Rumi

#6
I would institute a program of Kaizen—ongoing constant improvement.

Instead of being satisfied with "how it's always been," there is the opportunity to improve on "even the best." If we settle for less than excellence, we will get less than we are willing to settle for in the first place. The quest for improvement is a learned habit: The way we do anything is the way we do everything; the key is to improve ALL THINGS.

"Perfection is not attainable, but if we chase perfection we can catch excellence."
—Vince Lombardi

#7
I would give more and take less.

The ultimate self-gift is to give to others. After we attain all those benchmarks we have worked diligently to achieve, we come to the realization that the true value was in the journey, not the destination. As educators, shepherding our flock (students) to the immeasurable pleasure of connecting with great music makes us the wealthiest of all.

"The things you do for yourself are gone when you are gone, but the things you do for others remain as your legacy."
—Kalu Kalu

#8
I would teach with more enthusiasm, both content and context.

To be driven by enthusiasm is to demonstrate a strong excitement about our love of music. It's more than information sharing; rather, it's a commitment and dedication to connecting with a part of the mind, heart, and soul unknown by any other study—loving what we do, and doing what we love. THE GIFT OF MUSIC...priceless!

"Nothing right can be accomplished in art without enthusiasm."

—Robert Schumann

#9
I would always do more than is required...go above and beyond.

Meeting the standards is a worthy accomplishment. Setting the standards is the mark of a master. We are part of the most valued natural resource on the planet: HUMAN POTENTIAL. For those who make the most of life, "good enough" is *never* good enough. We must be inspired to be all we can be—and more.

"Doing what's expected of you can make you good, but it's the time you spend going above and beyond what is required that makes you great!"

—Josh S. Hinds

#10
I would express more thanks and offer more appreciation for anything and everything.

In the hurriedness to get to the next this-or-that, it is so easy to make the self-promise, "I'll thank them later"—but later never comes, and the opportunity to acknowledge another is lost in the sea of best intentions.

Recognizing/acknowledging others for their contributions is the greatest of all gifts—to be genuinely THANKFUL for what others have brought to life's table.

"Gratitude turns what we have into more. It turns denial into acceptance, chaos into order, confusion into clarity...it makes sense of our past, brings peace for today, and creates a vision for tomorrow."

—M. Beattie

As we know, hindsight is always 20/20. It is an easy exercise to "look back," to bet on the winning horse "after the race is completed." Likewise, one can peer into the rearview mirror of life and speak of wishes of grandeur, knowing there is no way to be held accountable or to make good on these bold claims. However, why be remiss of what we didn't do. Instead, institute these grand wishes STARTING RIGHT NOW.

The world is out there waiting...anytime you are ready.

CHAPTER 1

The Essential Element to a Successful Band:

The Teacher • The Conductor • The Director

The Leader

Tim Lautzenheiser

*"A teacher affects eternity; he can never
tell where his influence stops "*
—Henry Adams

The Art of Music and the Art of Teaching

The integration of substantive content and sensitive context is the key to success for any exemplary educator. In the field of music it is an absolute necessity. Bringing the data to the students is only one step in the growth process; presenting it in a fashion they understand and appreciate is equally challenging. The *art of music* combined with the *art of teaching* creates a forum of opportunity for every aspiring musician. It is necessary to bring both of these components to the rehearsal room if we expect to achieve our professional goals of *teaching music through performance in band*. This chapter is focused on the *contextual* aspect of the rehearsal: the role of the teacher/conductor.

The Band Director as a Leader

In today's educational system band directors are far more than trained musicians capable of conducting an array of beat patterns. Most of their school day is dedicated to a host of other responsibilities, and much-cherished podium time is all too brief; therefore, it is crucial to make use of every moment spent *rehearsing the band*. Time lost during rehearsals is lost forever, and the negative results of wasted time far exceed what is casually observed. Students often become frustrated and discouraged, and music rehearsals become an unpleasant experience rather than "the best time of the day." The band director is in a position to organize and lead students to new levels of musical understanding and expression. It is clear the band director must be a leader of people as well as a conductor of music. Blending both of these important aspects of teaching into one personality ensures a successful rehearsal for everyone involved. We cannot ignore the leadership attributes of the band director, but rather must emphasize them in ongoing professional development.

Traditionally, our colleges and universities have not required classes in the area of "people skills." It has always been assumed that a solid library of musical knowledge would suffice in the development of a successful teacher. In defense of these institutions of higher learning there is little if any time for elective courses if one is to complete the mandated requirements in a strict degree program. Additional classes outside the discipline of music are next to impossible. With the present requisites many students need five years to complete and receive their undergraduate diploma. In spite of this we must take note of ongoing research that specifically demonstrates the vital importance of various personality traits in determining success in the rehearsal classroom.

Research Emphasizes Personality Traits Needed for Success

In an ERIC document, *Characteristics of Effective Music Teachers* (University of Houston, No. ED 237 400), Dr. Manny Brand reported:

> Although possession of a high degree of musicianship was assumed, there are other essential qualities that a band director must possess:
>
> 1. Enthusiasm.
> 2. Warmth and personal interest.
> 3. A rehearsal technique combining clarity, brevity, fast pace, and variety.
> 4. A balance of praise and meaningful criticism.
> 5. A discipline technique focusing on communication.
> 6. A desire to improve and learn.

In a sequel to this study, Brand concluded:

> The ingredients of a master music teacher are: a sixth sense of understanding his or her students, pride in his or her remarkable competence, a fertile imagination, a theatrical flair, instructional

urgency, a drive to accomplish the highest musical goals, the drive to *work hard and obtain enormous satisfaction.*

Clearly this spotlights the band director as a teacher and communicator as well as a musician.

Mike Manthei of Valley City State University, Valley City, North Dakota co-wrote "A Preliminary Investigation into the Qualities of a Successful Band Director" with Ray Roth of Mackinaw City, Michigan, as part of the abstract sponsored by the American School Band Directors Association. The two reached a similar conclusion to Brand's. Quoting P. B. Baker's research in "The Development of a Music Teacher Checklist for Use by Administrators, Music Supervisors, and Teachers Evaluating Music Teaching," the ten most important characteristics of a successful music teacher/band director are:

1. enthusiasm for teaching and caring for students
2. strong, but fair discipline
3. observable student enjoyment, interest, and participation
4. communication skills
5. sense of humor
6. in depth musicianship
7. knowledge and use of good literature
8. strong rapport with the students, both individually and as a whole
9. high professional standards
10. the use of positive group management techniques

Manthei and Roth also bring the work of T. C. Saunders and J. L. Worthington in "Teacher Effectiveness in the Performance Classroom" (*Update,* 8 (2), 26–29) to their document with these revealing discoveries:

Saunders and Worthington found that aside from the high level of musical competencies, the successful music educator possesses four skills:

1. The ability to plan, both on paper and interactively, in the classroom setting.
2. The ability to format and pace lessons in a way that maximizes learning and minimizes frustration.
3. The ability to communicate with students in a variety of ways that enhance learning.
4. The ability to maintain a positive classroom atmosphere where expectations are high and students are constantly reinforced in their progress.

Certain similarities create a common theme in all of these data. Regardless of a researcher's findings, the qualities of enthusiasm, caring, communication, positive reinforcement, fair discipline, musical competency, and high professional standards serve as the suggested personality pillars of the successful band director.

From Research to Reality

- How does one develop these various personality traits?
- What techniques can be brought to the classroom setting that will guarantee a higher degree of musical learning?
- Which teaching skills need to be emphasized and which must be avoided?
- What are the responsibilities of the band director during rehearsals?

Personal development is a way of life for students of human potential. Much like practicing an instrument to attain mastery, outstanding educators are always fine-tuning their communication skills and seeking more efficient and effective ways of bringing the art of music to their students. The combining of the contemporary findings of leadership with traditional band directing has offered an exciting new frontier of possibilities. There is an ever-growing amount of data confirming the educator can program his or her personality to ensure a higher degree of success in daily rehearsals as well as performances. Just as a pilot is required to go through a pre-flight checklist prior to flying a plane, the band director should have a pre-rehearsal checklist prior to standing in front of his/her students:

1. Will my present attitude promote a positive learning atmosphere?
2. Are all my thoughts focused on creating a musical experience throughout the rehearsal?
3. Do I exemplify the standards of excellence I expect from my students?
4. Am I properly prepared to make the best use of time by highlighting the musical growth of every student?
5. Have I dismissed my own agenda of personal considerations so that rehearsal will be directed toward serving students in a disciplined format of measured learning?
6. Am I in touch with my philosophical mission of the importance of teaching music?

Success assumes an affirmative answer to these important pre-rehearsal questions, just as the pilot assumes his airplane is mechanically ready to endure the requirements of the flight. However, the mere process of reminding ourselves of the importance of our state of mind and the impact it will have on what can be accomplished during the upcoming rehearsal affords us the opportunity to avoid any damaging attitude we might inadvertently bring to the rehearsal setting. We demand total concentration from our musicians, and must therefore model this vital discipline. Pilots are not allowed to take off without a perfect score on their pre-flight checklist; directors should have a similar mandate before lifting students to new heights.

The Focal Point: Musical Prosperity for the Band

High-level achievement is attained when the synergy of students and director is centered on a common goal. This is accomplished through the band director's guidance based on the following four cornerstones of leadership effectiveness.

Make the Students the Emphasis of Your Teaching

The more you avoid relating suggestions, corrections, thoughts, and comments in *I/me* terms, the more students will assume personal responsibility. Emphasize *We/Us* and *You* in verbal exchange. For example:

> I think the trumpet phrase needs to have a gradual crescendo
> to establish more intensity prior to letter A. Do that for me.

becomes:

> Trumpets, *you* can generate some real excitement for *us* if you
> crescendo *your* line as you come up to letter A. *We're* counting on *you*.

Notice how the second instruction puts the responsibility on the players and offers them the chance to expressively contribute to the group, rather than simply "doing as they are told" to appease your request. They take ownership of the musical phrase and simultaneously become aware of their importance to their fellow musicians. The students are key in this process, for they bring life to the music. The director merely guides their energies toward achieving this mutually agreed-upon goal.

Explain Clearly What You Want from the Performers

Time is the director's most precious commodity and must be used judiciously. Any waste of time is a loss to everyone in the band. Communication skills—knowing what to say and how to say it—serve as the tools of every competent conductor. Avoid general comments that do not carry corrective instructions for improvement:

There is a balance problem in the brass.
That's unacceptable; let's do it again.

becomes:

Trombones, enter softly at letter G.
You must be able to hear the clarinets.

They now know exactly what to do, how to do it, and how to measure their success (they must hear the clarinets). All too often students want to fulfill the director's instructional expectations but are really not aware of what to do. In place of asking most students simply repeat their efforts until they either stumble accidentally on the right combination or just run out of time. Another cornerstone of leadership requires competent score preparation, which guarantees a more effective use of time.

Communicate throughout the Rehearsal

Communication is far more than words exchanged between playing segments. Communication can be verbal, visual, or tactile, and with music, band directors must incorporate intuitive connections with the musicians. Frequent eye contact is imperative—not only with first-chair players, but with every section and member of the band. If musicians are expected to watch the conductor, then the conductor must share this responsibility by visually communicating with the musicians. A picture is worth a thousand words, and facial gestures can bring new dynamics to every rehearsal. When students are aware of this ongoing forum of communication they begin to communicate actively with the conductor. Only then can we "make music" as opposed to "playing notes." If the director is focused only on the score, students will, likewise, focus only on their parts. The rehearsal then becomes a mechanical exercise, and the human factor—the truly expressive component—disappears. The greater the frequency of genuine director/student communication during the rehearsal, the greater the musical experience.

Take Responsibility for Every Condition in the Rehearsal

If there is a breakdown, an interruption, a discipline problem, or any other situation that threatens the rehearsal atmosphere, assume responsibility for it and move ahead. Stopping the band to justify, excuse, blame, or point out where someone is wrong (preventing the intended rehearsal plan from taking place) is almost always an infringement on valuable group time.

For example, if an emergency class meeting or an unscheduled athletic event removes students from rehearsal, embrace the situation and do not amplify the problem by wasting class time with the remaining musicians. Look for the possibilities the unexpected circumstances can provide (e.g., attention to certain sections of the music, listening to recordings, reviewing tapes, working on technique studies, and a myriad of other positive musical prospects). A verbal protest from the podium dwelling on the obvious encroachment on rehearsal time only adds negative fuel to the situation. Taking responsibility involves creatively using existing conditions to advance the cause of music for those students who remain, instruments in hand and eager to move ahead.

Intrinsic and Extrinsic Rewards

The joy of playing a musical instrument is an intrinsic experience. In every program there are extrinsic rewards, but it is vital that these bonuses be secondary in emphasis. If a student puts greater value on awards, chair placement, ratings, rankings, trips, or trophies than on musical experience, the *product* takes precedence over the *process*. However, if the pleasure of playing the instrument is the priority, extrinsic prizes are merely personal premiums along the pathway of artistic expression. Because of our often over-materialistic contemporary values, it is vitally important to repeatedly explain why music is an integral part of our lives and stress the importance of the *language of music*. The director must constantly point out the benefits of mastering technical skills in order to provide an extended musical vocabulary of self-expression. Music accesses a part of the mind unique to every individual. It is a language unto itself; music can only be explained by music. It is, quite literally, feeling described in sound. The more technique available to the musician—i.e., the higher the musical vocabulary—the more successful she will be in communicating her innermost feelings. Therein lies the benefit of dedicated practice.

Do not assume students will discover these *intrinsic dividends* on their own. Many promising young musicians give up studying music because they feel improperly compensated with extrinsic payoffs for their efforts and energies. For them, the success of their band experience is based solely on winning the contest, being selected as the soloist, appointed section leader, etc. They may be outstanding students committed to the band's success, but they consider playing their instrument as a means to the end; when the end does not provide a satisfying extrinsic reward, they choose not to continue their study.

In this case everyone loses, particularly the students that quit. In contrast, if intrinsic value is the mainstay of the band experience, extrinsic disappointments are far less damaging. Of course there will be setbacks, but they should not be devastating to an individual's relationship to band or music. In this case everyone wins, particularly the student who is ready to move on to the next level.

Motivation by Fear or Desire

What is motivation? The word derives from the Latin, *motere*, which means "lito motor" or "lito move." We envision the motivated student as one who moves forward in a positive direction. A motivated band is a group of young musicians moving toward a common goal of excellence.

How do we motivate students? Psychology tells us the only true motivation is *self-motivation*. Therefore, it is important to provide an environment in which students choose to move forward of their own volition rather than await some outside force to manipulate their behavior to accommodate the desired results. How can a director *light the fire* in young musicians?

Fear

Fear has long been an effective stimulant to alter behavior. There is no question that it plays on the basic human mechanism of survival. Pain, blame, guilt, and shame are certain to bring about predictable reactions; however, there are negative residual consequences to be dealt with following these actions. To remove fear as a form of behavior modification is unrealistic; however, a judicious use of this powerful tool is advised. It should be used sparingly and only in extreme circumstances. Rest assured, a time of healing will be necessary for both director and students once fear is purposely injected into the environment. When we are threatened, our natural reaction is to seek safety and choose the path of least resistance to avoid pain or embarrassment. An *extreme* option for student musicians would be to simply quit the band.

Desire

Desire does not carry with it the reaction-urgency of fear; however, the long-term pro-action effects are certainly more conducive to harmony, balance, blend, and mutual trust. These conditions serve as a better foundation for musical growth and development and support the ideals of a positive band experience for students. When students are *motivated* by an inner drive to reach the level of *desired* performance, the rehearsal atmosphere is dramatically shifted. Each student becomes his own source of power, allowing the director to focus that synergy—the combined energies of his students—to increase the pace of the learning process.

Time is not lost in disciplinary measures, but instead devoted to facilitating the path to musical prosperity. Students leave rehearsals enthused about band and are eager to recreate a similar set of standards in other facets of their lives as well as continue their musical journey, whether at home working on their individual parts or in the next scheduled rehearsal.

Creating a Positive Climate for Learning

Being in the band means devoting time to a common goal. It requires participants to relinquish much of their free time and/or fun time and reassign it to rehearsals. While many of their friends may enjoy the social benefits of adolescence, band students are fulfilling the requests of their and director. For a chosen few, the intrinsic payoff warrants the dedication of their efforts and energies. Others, however, seek additional dividends.

All students are not *intrinsically motivated*. But if they are properly trained, they will begin to comprehend a higher level of understanding and to wean themselves from extrinsic payoffs and enjoy music for the sake of music. Herein lies one of the most significant contributions a director can bring to any student: leading a child step-by-step to the joy of music. This metamorphosis is almost immediate for some, but requires extended patience with others. Persistence alone is omnipotent in this charge. What classroom conditions best serve this goal?

Condition 1: Safety

Is the rehearsal a *safe* place to reside? Abraham Maslow's scale of hierarchy is very clear concerning the importance of survival. He states that survival is the basic human need, quickly followed by the need for safety. If the atmosphere of the rehearsal is threatening, students will put a higher priority on survival (avoidance of pain) and safety (maintaining their dignity) than on extending their talents and skills for the common goal of the ensemble. If students and/or the director assume a defensive posture, it is certain to hinder the group's musical objectives.

Condition 2: Challenge

Learning is exciting. Master teachers are well aware of the enthusiasm generated in an exchange of knowledge where both student and teacher are challenged. There is a fine art to establishing challenging, attainable goals without overwhelming students with a barrage of information. Knowing each student learns at her own pace, the astute music teacher constantly regulates expectations to establish a challenge for gifted students while supporting the growth of those who learn at a slower pace.

Although it is difficult to explain how to establish this important teacher-student communication, it appears to fall in the realm of *intuitive sensitivity*. Experience itself is often the key to mastering this skill. Beware the temptation to focus only on fun and easy material; it is deceptive both to the director and students. Quality begets quality. The mind left unchallenged will search for another source of inspiration.

Condition 3: Encouragement

To encourage means to bring into the presence of *courage*. Although there are times when every band director must confront an uncomfortable situation, admonishment or discouragement should not be the theme of any rehearsal. In most cases students choose to participate in band above and beyond other academic requirements. Band often demands more of their time than other classes; therefore, it is important the band director becomes a source of honest encouragement.

Highlighting positive behavior is certain to develop a genuine sense of caring and sharing, and an atmosphere conducive to musical expression. Encouragement is a necessity. It is the fuel students seek in their journey through life, and can often be the deciding factor in lifting them from the depths of rejection to the infinite possibilities of musical mastery. Do not underestimate the importance of encouragement; use it often to unleash the power to move the group forward.

Effective Communication Translates to Effective Teaching

The world of high technology has dramatically shifted the world of communication for the upcoming generation. Educators must eagerly embrace this reality and adapt their communication skills to the modern-day language of computers, email, social networking, and more. The underlying theme of contemporary education is: *state the message in brief, understandable terms, avoiding extra verbiage.*

Students enter class with this fast pace in mind and are mentally geared to move quickly in accomplishing assigned tasks. The perceptive teacher will adjust his communication style to students' gait and take advantage of their ability to consume information at a high rate of exchange. This requires *energized* communication—the capability to engage students in the communication process to foster learning at the highest level.

Unlike in a traditional lecture procedure, the teacher instead opens the forum of idea exchange and encourages students to offer *their* thoughts and opinions. Proper teacher guidance and a prudent use of time are key elements in allowing students to "own the band" and feel a sense of personal contribution to the organization's success.

Inspired communication involves the love of students. If students are to be inspired, the teacher must be inspired. The influential conductor demonstrates love for teaching by becoming immersed in the daily agenda. Teaching is not an act, but rather an *interact*—an ongoing relationship with students.

The Master Teacher Perspective

> The good teacher tells.
> The excellent teacher explains
> and demonstrates.
> The master teacher inspires.
> —William Arthur Ward

Mr. Ward's words ring true in every aspect of our educational community; and perhaps they are *most* vivid in the world of music education. The role of the teacher, director, conductor, and/or mentor is to create a healthy atmosphere supporting the entire spectrum of music learning, music making, and music listening.

Analyze the wisdom of Ward's thoughts and apply it to your daily teaching habits in a fashion that benefits every one involved in the teaching-learning process.

The Good Teacher Tells

The very essence of education is "passing information from one source (the teacher) to another source (the student)." This represents the *what* in the curriculum. From *what* the dates are when Columbus landed in America to *what* is wrong with the intonation of the ensemble, we are all trained to bring to our classrooms and rehearsals rooms a library of evolving valuable data to expand and improve the lives of our students. Even as we continue our own education through workshops, graduate school, seminars, conventions, clinics, etc., we embellish our knowledge with everything from the latest statistics to new information embellishing our own understanding. Simply put, we know more *what*.

However, if all we do is *tell* our students this important data without holding them accountable for integrating it into their lives, we may be nothing more than another source of facts and figures. The overriding question is: "Is the material communicated in such a way that our students realize it can have a positive impact in relation to their well being?" Simply put, *does the teaching of the lesson have a lasting effect?* Most certainly the *what* is a crucial foundation block, but we cannot stop there.

The Excellent Teacher Explains and Demonstrates

The area of music education is one of the most exciting academic subjects begging for *explanation* and *demonstration*. Successful music teachers know it is the hands-on learning processes that are required for high-level achievement. We don't simply instruct *what* to do, but we show our students *how* to do it. We are participants as we sing along with them, conduct the ensemble, and serve as the accompanist. Not only do we explain how each vital skill is accomplished, we demonstrate the tone we are seeking, the needed style, the shape of the phrase, the music picture we are trying to paint.

The job requires so much more than simply "telling students *what* to do"; it is a matter of discovering countless ways to *explain* the various avenues of efficiently and effectively reaching the given goal. The *excellent* teacher goes to the next step by *demonstrating* what the final product should be.

The Master Teacher Inspires

To inspire is to establish a creative atmosphere in which students are "in the spirit" of the moment and can express themselves in such a way that they don't just *do* something, they *feel* something. It is the *why* of learning. It is taking the *what* combining it with the *how* and venturing into a new realm of *why*. When young musicians connect with *why* they are making music, then the motivation to strive for a higher level of proficiency takes on a whole new meaning.

> Music touches a part of our psyche that helps us regulate our lives. Music helps us understand and express our moods and attitudes. Music helps us reorganize our thoughts and feelings while keeping us on track. Music allows us to respond appropriately in social structure that is often confusing and complex. *Music makes us human.* The master teacher *inspires* us with this awareness.

As music educators, we have a direct line to the inner emotions of our students. So much of the school day is impressionistic (i.e., learning the information and replicating it on a test). But music is expressionistic. Each member of the class/ensemble has the opportunity to bring her emotions to create a musical portrait; each person has value and plays a key role in the creative process; and each person can contribute her *spirit* to the musical community.

Master teachers constantly challenge their budding young artists to explore *why* it is important to continue along the pathway of quality music-making.

The word *maestro* is taken from the Italian word *master*. As a maestro we can all be *master teachers*. We simply cannot forget to ask our students and ourselves *why?*

Seeing Beyond Notes:
Positive Growth and Development of Every Child

Ongoing research continues to evidence *why* music students are academically stronger, and why they are the high-level achievers in all aspects of education. The relationship is not accidental, coincidental, or even incidental. There is a definite, measurable link we can point to that clearly shows that music students have a distinct advantage over their counterparts who do not participate in a music program.

There are fundamental cornerstone reasons to include music as a part of every child's curricular blueprint. When we stand back and take a holistic view, the value of music learning takes on an enriched perspective.

The study of music provides learners the opportunity to grow in four key areas that enhance academic achievement:

Creativity

Creativity is the source of all possibilities. Musicians are constantly challenged to explore this area of the mind. Music opens new horizons and new possibilities through expanded thinking. Music study supports wonderment, imagination, appreciation, and sensitivity. Music allows us to experience creativity as an inventive thinking style.

Communication

Music is a language unto itself, and can only be explained by music. If we do not expose our students to music we deprive them of an array of personal understandings that cannot be found in any other part of the school curriculum.

Critical Assessment

Intelligence is the ability to process facts and respond according to a given situation. Emotional stability stems from the capacity to deal with life's many inconsistencies. To accomplish both, the individual must be able to access the cognitive (factual) and affective (emotional) sides of the mind. Music is one of the few academic disciplines that develops this ability and reinforces learning patterns to allow for greater critical assessment.

Commitment

Success is not measured by what we start, but rather by what we complete. Music study requires students to perform an entire composition from beginning to end; to complete a given task. The important qualities of tenacity and persistence establish habits for positive, productive living applicable in every situation.

As teachers we pledge our efforts to prepare our students for what lies ahead in their personal and professional journeys. In the process of preparing for a concert, sightreading new literature, teaching a musical concept, or listening to a quality performance, we help our students establish thinking habits that are immediately transferable to other academic areas, teaching the life-skills that will support their healthy and prosperous future.

It is apparent ongoing research spotlighting the benefits of music learning continues to confirm what we have long suspected; *music does make the difference.*

A Podium for Educational Success

Components for teacher success can be measured, taught, learned, and generally blended into every rehearsal. There is no mystery. What has been labeled as charisma is merely an execution of various behavior patterns carefully timed to focus young performers in a purposeful direction. The art of teaching, much like the art of music, is based on the strategic use of personality characteristics every educator can master.

This chapter would be incomplete without mentioning the elusive quality of *passion*. The great conductors are passionately devoted to their art form. They love the music, they love their students, and they are driven to share this passion with everyone. We authors tip our hats in thankful admiration and appreciation to exemplary models of teaching expertise. Outstanding mentors continue to set the standards for the profession as they passionately develop the leaders of tomorrow by *teaching music through performance in band* today.

CHAPTER 2

Successful Music Advocacy

Tim Lautzenheiser

Musical training is a more potent instrument than any other (for education)
because rhythm and harmony find their way into the inward places
of the soul, on which they mightily fasten, imparting grace, and
making the soul of him who is rightly educated graceful, or of him who
is ill-educated ungraceful.

··· Plato ···

Introduction

Within the last two decades—specifically starting in the early '80s—
music advocacy has come to the forefront of the music education world. The
focus is on the value of music in the educational development of our children.
Many professional leaders have contributed to the ever-growing wealth of
knowledge. Scientific research continues to point to music as a key factor in
the development the human mind. We no longer have to justify music with
platitudes or personal notions; the hard-copy facts and figures are now available. The horizon is bright for the world of music education, but only if we
fulfill our roles as the stewards of the good news, delivering it to the right
people and in the right context.

This chapter is not a definitive laundry list of specific suggestions or
instructions, such as developing the parent phone tree, sample letters to the
School Board, etc. Detailed advocacy kits are available and can be attained by
contacting the organizations listed at the end of the chapter. These advocacy
blueprints, offering success-proven techniques, are priceless and you are
encouraged to obtain them and share them with your music supporters. I see
your position as a leader, guiding and directing your music advocates and serving as an enthusiastic role model, much as you would direct your ensemble.
Therefore, this chapter is devoted to a more holistic approach to advocacy, an

overall perspective, a viewpoint that is specifically applicable to the music educator who is responsible for creating, developing, sustaining, and nurturing an advocacy organization.

The entire school year could easily be devoted to promoting the program, educating the administrators, informing the parents, and so forth. However, the primary responsibility of the music educator is to teach music. Keeping this in mind, and also being crucially aware of the importance of the advocacy component, "Successful Music Advocacy" approaches the advocacy responsibility through the eyes of the music teacher. For many it will be a shift in attitude, from an intense point of convergence based on creating a flawless performance to a larger perspective, one of comprehending and understanding that the process of learning music is more valuable than the final product. Strangely enough, when the mind is willing to accept this reality, the performance aspect of the ensemble inevitably improves. It is not just the awareness of the academic value of music, it is an acceptance of this reality and the integration of the knowledge (knowing) in the daily teaching habits. When this realization takes place, advocacy is no longer something we do, it is something we are.

The one common characteristic of programs of excellence is a strong and healthy advocacy constituent. The director/leader realizes the importance of music as an academic core subject and insists on sharing the information with everyone who has a vested interest in the music program, and, likewise, makes certain everyone is aware of their vested interest.

As a suggestion to the reader, do not simply peruse the chapter looking for some quick-fix solution or the hopeful discovery of a cute idea guaranteed to generate excitement about the band. You will be sorely disappointed. Read a paragraph and then apply it to your situation, reframe it to fit your needs, let it simmer in your mind, then reread it and mentally outline how you could adopt and adapt the information to benefit your program. Come back to the chapter time and time again; it is a reference, not a patented prescription.

Above all, approach the material with an open mind. In all too many instances we have become our own worst enemy by our unwillingness to shift, change, and conform to the present-day educational perspective. We, as music educators, offer students the most valuable educational training in the school; we give students the tools to manifest success in every phase of their lives. It's time to share the good news, to let our words accompany our music, and let the world know about the immeasurable value of music education through "Successful Music Advocacy."

Successful Music Advocacy: Communication Is the Answer

Educational reformation is a way of life in the American society. Politicians are eager to include education as a mainstay of their campaign platforms. Teachers know the curriculums must be in constant transition to accommodate the ongoing growth of modern technology. Parents are keenly aware of the importance of the learning atmosphere and are eager to see their children experience a positive learning culture. In the midst of this evolution, music, as well as the other fine arts, has come to the educational forefront and our nation is embracing the arts as a basic subject for every child.

In 1990 the Music Educators National Conference (MENC), the National Association of Music Merchants (NAMM), and the National Association of Recording Arts and Sciences, Inc. (NARAS) joined forces in establishing the National Coalition for Music Education. The first priority of the organization: to garner the support of people who are aware of the importance of music in our schools and begin a dialogue with state, regional, and district officials to promote music education and to avoid any kind of program reduction or omission based on budgetary decisions. The state and local coalitions are effective if they have strong leadership and the inclusive involvement of teachers, parents, administrators, and community patrons. As with any organization, success is measured by the strength of its membership.

Advocacy, by definition, means: "1. To push; 2. To bolster; 3. To further a cause." As teachers of music, band directors, we often allow advocacy responsibilities to slip to the bottom of the priority list. The daily responsibilities—ranging from selecting repertoire for the upcoming solo-ensemble festival to negotiating with the drama teacher for access to the concert hall—take precedence over any formally designed program of music advocacy. Directors contend that there simply is not enough time, and yet it is ever apparent that the outstanding band programs integrate advocacy in all aspects of the organization. It is not viewed as a separate responsibility, but is synthesized as part of the musical climate; it is a focused commitment, an ongoing sharing of the value of music in the growth of every child.

Granted, in years past, most colleges did not include a class in "Advocacy" as a requisite to the completion of the music degree. Even today advocacy is often combined with a general methods class, or included as an amendment to a preparatory class in student-teaching. The point is, many directors are clearly aware of the need for advocacy, but feel a great sense of inadequacy in creating, developing, and maintaining an ongoing advocacy agenda. As a result we are depriving the students, the parents, the school, the community, and ourselves of many benefits that add artistic richness to the musical experience. As with any template of educational growth, the greatest form of learning is by doing. We can no longer point the finger of blame at anyone; it is time to take action, shift the paradigm, and eagerly include advocacy in our teaching philosophies. It is time to do, to take action, to become active music advocates.

Music Advocacy: A Realistic Approach

When asked, "What is music advocacy?" thoughts of a school board meeting attended by several hundred supportive band parents with placards in hand loudly shouting their support for the director come to mind. While there have been such scenes (more for dramatic effect than for effective advocacy), this chapter is devoted to a more subtle and sophisticated approach focusing on pro-action rather than reaction. Instead of operating out of crisis mode to save the program from administrators' sharpened fiscal pencils, let us perceive advocacy as an opportunity to build alliances to secure the present program and become a participant in the future policy making. We must demonstrate a commitment to the ongoing exchange of data emphasizing the legitimacy of the core subject: music. Based on the amount of positive information available through the National Coalition Library (see reference page) and the ongoing research material surfacing daily through the efforts of MENC, NAMM, and NARAS, we are not lacking for convincing statistics highlighting the importance of music education; the challenge lies in the communication of the information. Any individual mildly interested in the education of our youth will quickly jump on the Arts Bandwagon after he/she has been exposed to the facts and figures concerning the impact of music in the human potential development process, i.e., learning. What is the most effective and efficient way to educate every one concerning the necessity of music for every child? That is the question: not what to do, but how to do it.

Advocacy Begins with the Director: You

Music advocacy begins with the director, it begins with a complete knowing and understanding of the mission, it begins with you. As stated in all the MENC materials, "Just as there can be no music without learning; no education is complete without music."[1] Herein lies the foundation of the music educator's professional mission statement: the belief/knowing that learning music is a part of every young person's birthright. It is easy to lose sight of this truth in the heat of performance deadlines; however this truth is the basis of every action taken, a fundamental truth that determines the prosperity of every program from beginning to end. We must first be believers before we can ethically engage others in our quest. "Why music? is not an unfair question, but one deserving of a clear, concise, easily understood answer.

PHILOSOPHICALLY:

1. Music is intrinsic, and in every individual; it is connected to the human spirit and creative mind. We cannot duplicate it through any other form of expression, we cannot quantify it. It exists for its own sake.

INTELLECTUALLY:

2. Music opens the mind. Ongoing brain research continues to link excelled learning skills with music. The breakthrough work of Dr. Gordon Shaw (University of California-Irvine) and his colleagues affirms every musician's inherent knowing, but (until now) not scientifically proven theory, of access to higher levels of creativity in every form of learning based on musical understanding.

EDUCATIONALLY:

3. Music teaches more than music. While these characteristics are not specifically tied to the study of music, they are a by-product of the process:

   A. The establishment of high achievement standards transferable to other academic subjects.
   B. Development of keen problem-solving patterns.
   C. Establishment collaborative teamwork habits through communication skills.
   D. Understanding flexible thinking and adapting the known to the unknown.
   E. Improvement of reading comprehension, motor proficiency, spatial awareness, and listening ability.
   F. Mastery of a given challenge while expanding the realm of understanding and pushing beyond self-inflicted limits (raising of personal standards).
   G. Increasing self-esteem, self-confidence, and self-discipline.

GLOBALLY:

4. Music is the universal language. The shrinking globe dictates the need for establishing relationships with every world culture. Cross-civilization communication continues to be at the forefront of our very existence. Music creates sensitive individuals dedicated to dispelling prejudices that jeopardize the harmony of mankind.

This is all well and good, but means little to present-day programs unless it is disseminated in an intelligent, understandable fashion to parents, school officials, political decision-makers, and even the students themselves. There is more to this music learning experience than renting an instrument and participating in band; it is focused on the preparation of the individual for a life of personal success and happiness.

The First Step:
To Convince Others, We Must First Convince Ourselves

The perspective of the educator who is a music advocate is shaped by a deep personal conviction. Just as the person of a given faith interprets the world through the filters of a chosen belief system, likewise the teacher who is a confirmed music advocate embraces his/her professional catalogue of responsibilities influenced by the realization that music education reaches far beyond producing a fine concert. It is not enough to bring the ensemble on stage and demonstrate beautiful intonation, clear articulation, and an expressive rendition of the music. While it is imperative we strive for these musical goals, they only represent one segment of the overall goal. The auditorium must be filled with enthusiastic parents, proud administrators, and appreciative community patrons. It requires more than just a few publicity tricks to guarantee a sold-out house; it is a reflection of those in attendance who understand, through careful educational guidance, the importance of music as an essential element of life. It will not happen by accident; it is the fruit of a solid, active advocacy program constantly fed by the director and his/her support team.

Communicating to the Right Audiences

The Students

The greatest stage for advocacy is the rehearsal room. Who needs to understand the value of music more than anyone? The students. It will be of little use to convince others if the students are not privy to the benefits of music as it relates to their development.

Speak to the students concerning music as an expressionistic language. School, for the most part, is impressionistic—an exercise in memorizing various bits of information in preparation for the test. However music offers the opportunity to involve the heart and mind in a process of personal expression, to reach beyond the notes on the page. Encourage the connection of the students' inner thoughts to the music, constantly remind them of the need to "be the music" and not just "play the music." The zenith experience for any musician is to be one with the music. With proper instruction this could easily happen at the beginning level of music learning with the first note, and it should. Advocacy, at the level of students, is supporting their love of music and their desire to continue their journey of self-exploration. Conversely, if the student associates band (orchestra, choir, etc.) with a negative connotation, then all other advocacy efforts are of little consequence. First and foremost, the students must sense the teacher's dedication to music as an art form.

The Parents

The parents are more than just a body of people who raise funds for additional equipment, or meet monthly for an update of the ensemble's planned activities. The parents have a vested interest in the program, and the director, in turn, has a responsibility to create an open line of communication that serves as a busy network of exchange relating the valuable impact music has on every student. Caution: when the parents/boosters are only an avenue to financial gains, the participation will be meager. If, however, the parent organization embraces the educational worth of music, the allegiance will evidence a notable increase in membership and active involvement.

Communication is the answer. It must be frequent, sincere, selfless, and dedicated to the parents' greatest concern: the welfare of their child. With the arrival of e-mail, the internet, web pages, etc., communication to an unlimited number of people is available at the touch of a computer key. Communication is not a luxury, it is a necessity. There is an endless supply of positive data ready to be shared with the parents; the challenge is to offer it to them in a user-friendly format. Communication is the answer and the key to all successful advocacy efforts.

Constantly reinforce the importance of music aside from the obvious; playing the clarinet, marching in the local parade, or performing at the annual holiday concert are tangible measurements of music education, but we know it is only the tip of the iceberg. Remind the parents that music builds critical thinking skills, prepares students for the rigors of higher education, invigorates the process of learning, and pushes the mind to an advanced level of competence. The excitement of the concert will be short lived, but the awareness of the long-range advantages of music education will serve as a strong influence for future parental decision making.

The Administrators

Administrators, in almost every case, are former classroom teachers. They made a career choice to contribute to the education of children by assuming a set of new challenges. Like everyone, their administrative choices are based on available information. With rare exception the administrator will do what is best (in his/her perception) for the positive educational growth and development of the students. To assume the administrator is aware of the benefits of music education is professional naiveté. In many cases the principal, supervisor, superintendent, etc., only sees/evaluates the results of the music classes at a basketball game (the pep band), at graduation (the band without seniors), or the July Fourth parade (summer band with the new eighth graders). This is hardly a fair assessment of a teacher's academic worth. In many instances the music wing of the school is at the opposite end of the building; administrators and directors can go weeks, even months without seeing one another. This creates, by proximity, a void in communication; remember, communication is the answer.

Paying frequent visits to the administrator's office offering important music information is as vital as tuning the band before the rehearsal begins. Inviting the administrators to come to class (rehearsal) is always an eye-opening experience for all. Student leaders can serve as messengers of good news concerning the program by requesting monthly update meetings with administrators. Parents should be encouraged to seek various ways to include administrators in the booster meetings and events. Create a partnership with the administrator and the music program; by doing so the administrator becomes a music advocate via the inclusion process.

The Colleagues

The word "colleague" generally refers to music colleagues. Consider other teachers in the school as your advocate-colleagues. The human is infamous for polarizing with its own ilk or likeness, and education is no exception; English teachers talk to one another, coaches stick together, elementary educators chat with other elementary teachers, and music educators are no different. It is difficult to garner the support of interdisciplinary colleagues if we only communicate with other music educators. Advocacy is based on outreach. It is difficult to convince anyone of anything if we wait for people to come to us. We cannot afford to idly sit in the music office hoping others will have a sudden artistic revelation. When a music teacher says, "There isn't enough time to get to know the other teachers in the school," it demonstrates a shortsightedness that builds a certain communication barrier. In truth we must know every teacher in the school; these colleagues are key members of the advocacy team.

Over thirty percent of college graduates participated in their high school music program. One could easily conclude that one out of every three teachers in the school has participated in band, orchestra, or choir. It is time to bring them back to music and they will become new advocate-leaders for other faculty members. Invite your colleagues to play in a concert, work with a sectional, travel with the ensemble, be a soloist at a concert, serve as the announcer, become part of the music program. The dormant but enthusiastic adult musician is simply waiting for an opportunity to rejoin the band. It is very likely that a third of the school faculty are already music advocates; tap this powerful source of support.

The Community Leaders

It is true: if the quality of student education diminishes, the community's life-style will also diminish. The Athenians were well aware of the crucial balance between education and community welfare (music was also a required subject in the Greek educational system). Our forefathers insisted on an education for every child (represented by our public schools) for they knew it would secure America's position as a world leader. This theme is evident at the national, state, regional, and local levels. In smaller communities, the music teacher is the focal point of arts education, and the people of the community look to this individual (you) for advice, direction, and all expertise dealing with music. They must be included in the communication loop; otherwise they will assume music education is what they hear on the radio and see on television. These people are taxpayers, voters, members and friends of the Board of Education, golfing partners with your administrators and colleagues. The conversations they have with their friends and acquaintances must positively support music education, and the most persuasive voice in the community is the music director.

The opportunities for community participation are endless, literally at the limits of the imagination, but the thoughts must be directed to mine the gems hidden within the local population. Does the editor of the area newspaper play trombone? Is the grocery store owner a percussionist? Did your doctor, minister, insurance agent sing in a choir? Even if they do not want to perform, rest assured they will want to contribute in some fashion, for they know the value of a solid music education. Reach out to them and invite them to be an active member of your advocacy organization; they will eagerly join.

Most successful business people are eager to support education. They realize their own achievements are a product of their knowing, their education. You can count on them for contributions of financial support if you can demonstrate through advocacy what their help will mean to the youth of the community. Do not expect the potential philanthropists to seek out the music program; you must go to them. It is the responsibility of the music advocate to make the first move. Communication is the answer.

The General Public

Contrary to popular thought, the general public is very much in favor of music education. The overwhelming opinion of American people is very pro-music, pro-art. Karl Bruhn, former Director of Market Development for the National Association of Music Merchants, was a key figure in the establishment and organization of the National Coalition. In one of his many essays, "On Preaching to the Choir: The Good News and the Bad News," he states (in reference to the 1992 Harris poll prepared at the request of the American Council for the Arts): "More than nine out of ten polled, for example, said it was important for children to learn about the arts and to develop artistic interests in school." He goes on to say:

> What the results of the Harris poll really mean is that we have to redouble our efforts to make sure the right message gets to the right people. We have to tell the decision makers not just that education in music and other arts has intrinsic value, or that it is the "right thing to do," but this is what the people in their community and in their state—in large numbers—want their children to learn.[2]

Much of the groundwork is in place for advocacy; the missing link to the puzzle appears to be leadership at the local level. Advocacy begins with the music educator. While it is possible to delegate individual duties along the way, the advocacy wellspring is, and will always be, part of the mission of every music teacher. There is an army of support ready and eager to come forward. They are already convinced the arts/music have a place in the educational framework of our youth. Take the lead, become the focal point for pro-music advocacy within your community.

Guidelines to Successful Music Advocacy

The first part of this chapter has been devoted to the big picture of music in our schools: the whys and wherefores of music education. Where do we start? What is the first step? What are the key factors in making certain the invested time and energy produces the results needed? Of course every individual will discover his/her particular style of advocacy as time goes on, but there are many tried-and-true road signs that will aid along the advocacy journey.

Cooperation, Not Competition

Never promote the music program at the expense of another organization. Music must stand on its own and should not compete with any other aspect of the school's programs. Creating a situation where an individual is forced to choose is not only unfair to the one who chooses, but has no educational foundation. When an either-or situation appears, the students will always lose. Music advocacy is a benefit to the entire school and community; it must live in harmony with the existing curriculum.

Advocacy Is Student-Oriented

Music education is centered around students, children, the musicians. If the theme of the advocate is self-serving, then the charade will be short lived, as it should be. While there may be teaching positions retained or even added because of advocacy programs, this certainly is not the priority-theme. The emphasis is music education for every child. It must not be disguised to save one's job or buy a new amplification system for the jazz band; it must be focused on the academic importance of arts education. It is about students, not adults.

Think "Everyone Is a Musician"

Potentially every student in school could be in the band, the orchestra, and/or the choir. When discussing music advocacy, everyone is a student, not just those enrolled for the semester. Should we be satisfied with the participation of ten percent of the school? Are we simply trained to accept the fact that only a chosen few will be involved in music? Should we be content with enough good players for one showcase group? Why are we limiting our scope?

Are we the living echo of "it's always been this way"? Every student walking the hallways of the school is a potential music-maker. Bringing this attitude to advocacy makes the message very potent.

Developing Relationships Is Advocacy in Action

"What are your thoughts about the importance of music education for our children?" Ask the question, then listen. (Remember, you wanted their opinion; they didn't inquire about yours.) You don't have to agree or disagree, simply discover what people know or don't know about music education. Thank them and extend genuine appreciation for their time. Follow up with a short note of acknowledgment and include some of the latest information about music research. Developing trust relationships is the basis for group support.

Share Music with Everyone

When a member of your musical ensemble performs, it's newsworthy. When the band plays, everyone needs to know. Publicity is often an afterthought. Telling the students to "bring parents to the concert" will not pack the house. Studying and knowing the musical scores is crucial in conducting a successful performance; creating and developing the audience is equally as crucial. One cannot be at the expense of the other; both exist in an exemplary music program.

It is not essential to engage in every aspect of the publicity campaign, but it is necessary to guide those who are in charge and reinforce the theme of music education as the foundation of the program. They must be aware of the inherent values that music offers the performer as well as the listener. It is more than just creating a large audience, it is the chance to involve more people in the support of music.

Open the Forum

Invite guests to share in the musical harvest. Add a local politician to the concert to welcome the audience and speak about the importance of the arts. Bring other music teachers in the system and in the area to conduct and perform. Acknowledge in the written concert program and at the performance the music teachers who were part of the lives of the students on stage. Extend appreciation to everyone who plays a role in the music community; it is amazing what will get accomplished when others receive the credit.

Learn, Learn, Learn

It is tempting to slip into the we've-always-done-it-this-way rut. Life becomes a series of habits and complacency takes over creative thinking. For your own continuing growth, invite a respected colleague to review your program and make suggestions for future growth and improvement. Talk honestly and openly with your principal, supervisor, superintendent and mutually agree upon a plan to accomplish short-range and long-range goals. Open your ears to the thoughts and opinions of your students and be appreciative of their candor, even though you may not agree. Continue your professional growth by attending workshops, reading professional journals and magazines, and—above all—listening to outstanding music performed by the finest musicians of the day. Keep your ears, your eyes, your thoughts, and your mind open. And, above all, enjoy the journey. We live in a country that knows the importance of the arts; we have only scraped the surface of possibilities. The opportunities are infinite. Communication is the answer. Let the music begin.

Strike Up the Band!

Notes

1 "Growing Up Complete, The Imperative for Music Education," (Music Educators National Conference, Reston, Virginia, March, 1991), p. 37.
2 Bruhn, Karl T., "On Preaching to the Choir: The Good News and the Bad News," Southwestern Musician (Texas Music Educators Association, March, 1993), p. 60.

CHAPTER 3

The Band Director as a Leader

Tim Lautzenheiser

Introduction

Successful band programs are a reflection of a successful band director. It is rare to find one without its predictable counterpart. Higher education continues to search for the ideal preparatory curriculum that offers the expectant music educator the necessary library of knowledge required to create and nurture a quality band program; however, the development of the leadership personality of the band director continues to be an equal challenge. We know that teaching context is equally as important as the curriculum content. With that in mind, this chapter is devoted to a bird's-eye view of two leadership styles as they impact the teaching/learning environment.

The Band Director as a "Leader"

We would all agree that the responsibilities of a successful band director extend far beyond the podium. Aspiring young music educators are required to study all aspects of music history, theory, form and analysis, composition, rehearsal techniques, orchestration, curriculum development, acoustics, and a host of related subjects. The development of the band director as a "leader" is often overlooked or discounted as an area outside the realm of musical expertise needed to be a professional success.

Times have changed. The inner desire to participate and contribute to a quality ensemble is still a high priority of young music makers; however, the process to achieve this end has shifted dramatically over the last three decades. In the past, students were expected to be obedient, focused, and dedicated to excellence. If they did not oblige, strong disciplinary measures were often brought to bear. Such extrinsic, imposed control became the admired standard as a requisite for musical success. An all-or-nothing approach is not as well received by today's more worldly students. Although the quest for musical excellence is still at the forefront of their desired goals, the journey (process) is equally as important as the destination (product). There is a shift from the authoritarian band director to the music educator who is concerned about the overall welfare of each musician while maintaining the group's high artistic standards, both on and off the podium.

There is an important difference that exists between the *demand* for excellence and the *desire* for excellence. While both avenues may produce the same results, the impact on the participants often dictates their future commitment to the ensemble/band. For example, a director-enforced rehearsal atmosphere can (and often does) produce an outstanding ensemble; the demand for excellence is recognized by the students/members and they behave accordingly; often this is to avoid any negative reprimands generated by the director. The second example is a student-imposed disciplined atmosphere leading to a similar quality performance; however, the rehearsal environment is a reflection of both the musicians' and the director's agreed-upon intent. Moreover, the desire for excellence shifts more of the responsibility back to the members of the group.

In reviewing these two examples, we (as music educators) must ask, "Which environment develops the lifelong musician?"

A Demand for Excellence

Noted author/psychologist, Dr. Abraham Maslow, points to survival as the primary human need on his Scale of Hierarchy. When an individual is confronted with a perceived threat, the initial reaction is to survive at all costs. In other words, the person chooses whatever path ensures ongoing survival. Based on this premise, behavior modification can be determined or controlled by pain, shame, guilt, and/or blame. Submission takes precedence over confrontation; the follower simply submits to the pressure rather than risk the consequences of challenging the authority figure and the outcome associated with insubordination. In a classroom setting, we can extrinsically (and expediently) motivate students by employing management/leadership tactics that threaten perceived survival (e.g., avoidance of pain, embarrassment, etc.).

A Desire for Excellence

A desire for excellence finds the source of motivation within the followers/students. Rather than the director being responsible for the rehearsal climate, the students determine the organization's level of expectation. They are given more freedom concerning appropriate behavior, individual commitment, disciplinary standards, and so forth. Generally, it takes more time to achieve the same level of musical performance as a director-controlled ensemble since time-consuming group choices now become a part of the learning process. For many directors, the benefits gained by sharing the ownership of the program are more important than the satisfaction of having ultimate control.

Arguably, there are merits to both styles of leadership, classroom management, and teaching philosophies. To suggest there is only one acceptable route to musical excellence is short-sighted; however, by understanding the extremes of the teaching/leadership processes, we increase our options for creating the best atmosphere to support our educational/musical goals.

As a reference point, let us label our two teaching styles as follows:

1. Demand for excellence (director control-oriented)
2. Desire for excellence (student control-oriented)

(Author's note: To avoid being caught in the semantics of the words desire and demand, we all know every fine music educator teaches from a position of desire; we also know every successful student is demanding in his/her personal learning habits. Demand and desire stand as equal partners in the growth/success journey. We are focusing on the source of application: is it director generated or student generated? Or what combination will best serve the journey/process and the destination/product?)

A *demand* for excellence reflects a more traditional style of leadership. The focus is on "finding and fixing" what is wrong, and the extremes justify the means in accomplishing the desired results. A *desire* for excellence is a more contemporary style of teaching/leadership. The focus is on an agreed alignment of the members to contribute to the purpose and vision of the organizational goals, with the means often taking a higher precedent over the extremes.

The consummate leader/teacher/director does not necessarily prescribe to one particular style, but blends both to accommodate the given situation(s). By reviewing the characteristics of *demand* and *desire*, we can gain a better perspective of what will best serve our programs.

Comparison of Teaching Styles

FINDING SOLUTIONS:
Director A is answer/tell-oriented:

Director A feels the need to answer every question and give specific instructions to the members of the ensemble. This guarantees the situation outcome and avoids the confusion associated with lack of direction. It can also thwart creative problem-solving and decision-making offered by the students.

Students become accustomed to the director "being in charge," and they wait obediently for the next directive.

Positive value:

It offers quick, instructive directions for problem-solving.

Negative potential:

Students rely totally on the director and avoid personal initiative.

Director B is question/listen-oriented:

Director B does not feel a need to "have all the answers," but focuses the students on finding their own solutions. While this leadership style develops group responsibility, it can consume an inordinate amount of time. Many possible solutions will be tried before an acceptable idea surfaces. The director must offer guidance and structure for the students.

Positive value:

A source of creative ideas comes forth and the students learn and understand the pros and cons of decision-making.

Negative potential:

Forward momentum can be lost because of a lack of unified direction. Without proper coaching, students can become frustrated because they simply don't know what to do, how to do it, or why they should do it.

DECISION-MAKING:

Director A makes all decisions:

Director A looks at every choice with a careful analysis of how it will impact the organization. Top-down decision-making is the overall mode of operation. Even though there may be various student leaders/officers, etc., the "final call" is made by the director. In truth, this style of leadership is a combination of leader-manager; assigning, doing, and evaluating is a function of the director.

Positive value:

There is total control and complete understanding of every programmatic detail.

Negative potential:

An excessive amount of time is spent micro-managing, checking and re-checking every choice/decision while being the only answer source for the group.

Director B empowers students to make decisions:

Director B assigns given tasks to the students in an effort to develop a sense of organizational ownership while tapping the creative thoughts of the participating students. Members are challenged to resolve their own problems and are encouraged to learn by trial and error. The director monitors the progress of the students as they explore choices and seek solutions; ongoing assessment and course correction is required.

Positive value:

> This method of leadership helps access the wealth of knowledge and creative energy within the ensemble.

Negative potential:

> Some students take action before having proper data; their unbridled enthusiasm can take the group off course. Communication can become easily fragmented.

MOTIVATION:

Director A pushes the ensemble for results:

Director A gets behind the organization and drives the members forward as they move to a higher standard of musical performance. When the group does not respond, the *demand* for excellence becomes the primary focal point and the leader/director counters by pushing with more force. The power source is the director; the emphasis is on the hard issue – the musical product.

Positive value:

> When there is progress slow-down, the director can take immediate steps to quickly reverse the cycle.

Negative potential:

> Students are only motivated to perform at the request/demand of the director. Extrinsic motivation is often seen as required for musical success.

Director B pulls the ensemble toward a vision:

Director B is postured in front of the program, ensemble, and students to create a visionary goal. When the group does not respond favorably, the *desire* for excellence becomes the primary focal point and the leader/director counters by focusing the attention of the group members on their chosen goal. The emphasis is on the soft issue – the people rather than the product. The students are challenged to rise to the occasion and urged to understand their responsibility to take charge of their musical destiny.

Positive value:

> The source of energy lies within the students; goal achievement is attained as a result of their contribution; intrinsic motivation is developed. Director-student communication is expanded, enhanced, and creates group synergy.

Negative potential:

> If the students do not recognize their need to assume this responsibility, forward momentum is halted. An excessive amount of valuable time can be lost.

PROGRAM PACING:
Director A has definite opinions:

Director A maintains forward progress by relying on the tried-and-true ideas and thoughts that have stood the test of time. While there is always room for growth, there is a certain black-and-white approach that keeps the program and the students well within the dictated, approved boundaries of the director. The future of the program is predictable since it reflects the opinions and thoughts of the director.

Positive value:

People know what behavior is appropriate and they usually adapt quickly. There is no second guessing or wondering how to interpret the directions of the leader/director/teacher.

Negative potential:

Opinions are not challenged or questioned; thus, alternative options are rarely explored. People simply wait for instructions and obey without going through a detailed thought process for themselves.

Director B is open minded and invites new data:

Director B also has opinions, but they exist as an avenue to further exploration of possibilities. "Either/or" gives way to "How can we make it work?" The line of right or wrong is flexible, and the thoughts and opinions of Director B are always in transition. Having an open ear encourages students to express their ideas without fear of appearing inferior or unknowing.

Positive value:

Students eagerly share their thoughts and ideas, realizing they can con tribute to the texture of the program. Rather than repress concerns, students bring them to an open forum where there can be discussion and resolution.

Negative potential:

Students who need clear and concise directions are often confused by the ongoing shifts in program adjustments. They can easily be discouraged and frustrated by the lack of direction-definition if the director does not communicate the given changes and the reasons for those changes.

LEADERSHIP POSTURE:
Director A demonstrates a mode of self-protection:

As part of the control posture, Director A never allows a situation where there will be any kind of threat to his/her position or leadership stance. The system is designed to maintain the security of the director and to avoid any questioning of the dominance of the leader. There is a clear-cut division between student, teacher, administrator, parent, etc.

Positive value:

Although this may be interpreted as a self-serving characteristic, it can help directors/leaders move ahead without fear of being undermined by others in the organization.

Negative potential:

Students/members begin to reflect the self-protection theme and start building their own walls of defense to guard their personal interests. Honest communication begins to decrease between director and students.

Director B is more relaxed in the interpretation of position importance:

Director B avoids self-protection to demonstrate a higher level of self-confidence. Time and energy that might be spent protecting the position of director is devoted to the inclusion of others to share the various responsibilities connected with decision-making and program mission.

Positive value:

The students connect to a common vocabulary and interpret the director's open style as a pathway to mutual growth for everyone.

Negative potential:

If the director doesn't maintain a professional posture, the lines between student and teacher become blurred and many students cannot decide what is and what isn't acceptable behavior.

PROBLEM IDENTIFICATION AND CORRECTION:

Director A focuses on problems and is quick to correct them:

Director A has a radar-keen sense when it comes to identifying problems. The never-ending goal of solving every problem to attain perfection is at the top of the priority list. The ability to analyze every minute infraction and give specific directions for correction ensures ongoing improvement.

Positive value:

The director can use knowledge, experience, and a library of solutions to push the ensemble forward at a very fast pace. Veteran teachers can even predict problems before they occur and help the students avoid potential breakdowns.

Negative potential:

The emphasis is always in a "fix and repair" mode. If there are no evident problems, some must be created to accommodate this style of teaching/leadership. Rarely is there the opportunity to feel a sense of personal satisfaction and enjoy a group celebration.

Director B highlights building strengths by learning from mistakes:

Director B recognizes problems but encourages, leads, and demonstrates "how" to fix them and "why" the correction needs to happen. Instead of giving the students the answer, Director B will go through an educational exchange allowing the students to contribute to the improvement pattern while offering creative counsel to find the solution.

Positive value:

The members of the group begin to model self-responsibility and share the responsibility of critical correction. The director can now dedicate more energy to other aspects of musical growth.

Negative potential:

The director may assume the students have proper information to complete the correction process while the members of the group either may be waiting for instructions or simply do not know what to do or how to do it, which leaves the ensemble at a musical standstill.

A Template for Success

As we examine today's most successful directors/leaders, there are some obvious key characteristics that serve as the foundation's cornerstones that we can highlight and adapt to our own situations:

1. Present an inspiring and compelling mission:

Instead of merely "working to get better," outstanding directors constantly communicate the group's shared goals. While elevating the musical standards, they create an ongoing awareness of various ways to support the ensemble's vision. The long-range goals are always at the forefront of their communication, thus allowing the students to focus on the self-imposed behaviors required to achieve the organizational mission.

2. Demonstrate proven disciplines necessary to create group synergy:

The emphasis is on the "power of the people" rather than the strict authoritarian rule of the director. The energy of the students serves as the fuel for forward motion. Discipline is an outgrowth of the commitment of the group members; instead of "being told what to do," the students are challenged to develop their own parameters of behavior that will support the program from bottom to top.

Positive discipline renewal comes from an ongoing series of group questions such as:

- "What is working well for us and why is it working?"
- "How could we better serve the people, the group, the goals?"
- "What behavior will best support those around us?"
- "What behaviors are counterproductive? How can we alter them?"

Blame is discouraged; solution options are encouraged.

3. Put people first:

The young musicians, students, members of the group are the source of unlimited growth and development. It becomes the director's responsibility to unleash the knowledge, creativity, and talent inherent in every member. This requires an ongoing interaction among everyone associated with the program; an open and honest line of communication confirms the director's concern for the welfare of the musicians.

4. Model a high degree of self-responsibility:

The "Do as I say, not as I do" theme is not as effective in today's educational setting. It is important for the director to take responsibility for mistakes and share credit for successes. Modeling is still the most potent method of teaching/leading; therefore, it is imperative that the successful director demonstrates trust, appreciation, caring, and concern. The master teacher/educator understands that it is not necessary to have the answers to all questions, but that strength often comes from saying, "I don't know. Let's find the answer together."

5. Have high expectations for results:

The modern-day successful band directors are both people-oriented and results-oriented. They focus on the dual task of "taking care of people" and "creating results through those people." While accepting who people are, they do not accept behavior that does not support the goal of quality. This delicate balance is an ongoing learning process for the director and the ensemble; it is constantly changing, shifting, becoming.

Creating a Culture of Quality through Leadership/Modeling

One of the most difficult challenges directors face has little to do with the actual teaching of music; it concerns the establishment of a positive learning atmosphere that encourages the members of the group to contribute without fear of embarrassment, reprimand, pain, etc. If the students assume a defensive posture to protect themselves, it becomes impossible to access their creative potential; however, if the director consistently models a forward-focused discipline, a remarkable shift in attitudes, energy, and performance can be felt. There will be a dramatic improvement recognized in every facet of the rehearsal climate and performance achievement.

Conclusion

The style of teaching we choose is a very personal decision; it usually is an outgrowth of our own educational background. "We don't teach as we're taught to teach; we teach as we are taught." We tend to replicate the style of our most influential mentors as well as draw on our own learning experiences as the foundation of our teaching approach.

As we add more data to our collection of teaching tools, it becomes advisable to expand our leadership skills accordingly. Yet this area of personal growth seems to be the most difficult, the most challenging and, often (unfortunately), the most ignored. It takes an open mind, a willing spirit, and an accepting attitude; it is simply easier and less threatening to add more curriculum content without shifting the teaching context. However, if we expect our students to reach a higher level of musical expertise, we are responsible for modeling the characteristics needed to achieve this end – and this involves change.

We all know what changes need to be made to advance our band programs, whether it is larger budgets, better schedules, more administrative support, greater community awareness, or a host of other possible factors. However, these changes will not take place until we change. If, in fact, the band program is a reflection of the band director, then to manifest changes in the program we must first manifest changes within ourselves. And it is more than changing the surface behavior; it involves a rigorous identity review and a constant evolutionary improvement of our teaching philosophies.

In Stephen Covey's popular book, *The Seven Habits of Highly Effective People*, he writes, "Change – real change – comes from the inside out. It doesn't come from hacking at the leaves of attitude and behavior with quick fix personality ethic techniques. It comes from striking at the root – the fabric of our thought, the fundamental, essential paradigms, which give definition to our character and create the lens through which we see the world."

In other words, the responsibility for creating an environment that supports ongoing positive growth and development is squarely on our shoulders. We must provide and model the positive disciplines we expect of our students and supporters. When we do so, the group begins to change; more and more people begin to follow the leader (the band director), and a noticeable transformation takes place.

Perhaps the most important question we must ask is, "What do I want the band to be?" Whatever answers are generated by this question can be transferred to the correlating question, "What are the characteristics of the band director who can create this envisioned program?" It is not enough to simply answer these introspective questions; we must become our answers.

Whether a *demand* for excellence or a *desire* for excellence; there is one very obvious commonality: *excellence*. The journey to excellence requires a delicate balance of demand and desire. If the destination is reached at the expense of the group members, we must re-evaluate our leadership style. If excellence is experienced throughout the learning process, the benefits enjoyed by everyone are immeasurable.

In the words of Carl Jung, distinguished psychologist/philosopher, "The human is doomed to make choices." As directors, teachers, leaders, the choices we make shape the lives of every musician in the band.

Strike up the band....

CHAPTER 4

The Selection and Development of Effective Student Leaders

Tim Lautzenheiser

"You cannot teach a man anything.
You can only help him discover it within himself."
--- Galileo ---

Author's Note

Over the past two decades, I have enjoyed the tremendous opportunity to present leadership seminars to students, teachers, administrators, and business professionals throughout the nation. Leadership, unlike many disciplines, is constantly shifting, evolving, changing, and "becoming." In fact, the more we learn about the art of leadership, the more puzzling and mysterious it becomes. Modern-day leadership experts continue to highlight the importance of developing *leadership values* along with the understanding of systemic leadership techniques. The shift from *people control* to *group empowerment* is a common theme in today's contemporary leadership training; ultimately, the welfare of the people is the primary concern. The *process* becomes equally as important as the *product*.

Bands (music programs) are perfect settings for leadership training. The band culture represents a microcosm of the community environment and requires a cast of leaders to teach, explain, create, and serve the various members of the musical society. Student leaders are not a luxury but a necessity; therefore, the selection, training, and guidance of these young leaders is a crucially important aspect of every band director's daily responsibility. The following chapter is a leadership blueprint dedicated to helping you and your students develop a positive and productive student leadership curriculum that will serve the band in achieving excellence in every aspect of the band program.

By design, the following pages are sequenced in subchapters:

Character Traits of a Student Leader
A view of the six character traits desirable (and necessary) for the selection of the leader candidate are presented.

A Paradigm Shift for Today's Leaders
The emphasis on intrinsic motivation as opposed to extrinsic rewards becomes the charge for every young leader; to this end, the expectations of the leader are outlined in a clear and concise approach.

The Personal Values of a Student Leader
Simply put, *giving* and *forgiving* become the key factors in creating a safe, encouraging, and challenging environment to foster the growth of the members of the band.

Choosing Leaders: Maturity Is the Key
If there is one absolute in the leader selection process, it is the measurement of the candidate's maturity. Is he/she prepared to assume the additional responsibilities and assigned tasks?

Solution-Driven Leaders: The Ultimate Choice
Many people can recognize the problem, the successful leader is the person who offers the solution. It is vitally important the student leader understands that the key to quality is determined by the collective work ethic of his/her followers.

Reading all of the subchapters at one time may not be as valuable as looking at each one as a separate template of leadership training. May I suggest you have your student leader candidates study these various areas of leadership development as they launch on their leadership journey; the benefactors of this exercise will be *everyone*.
Strike up the band!

Character Traits of a Student Leader

Student leaders are no longer a luxury in our educational world but rather a necessity, particularly in the field of music. Any successful ensemble is made up of a strong director and a committed group of responsible and dedicated student leaders. We count on these extraordinary young people to offer their time and energy in the ongoing growth and development of our programs; without them, much of the daily work simply would not be completed.

Students are usually eager to assume the leadership roles, but are they *capable* of assuming the responsibilities that accompany the real leadership agenda? Do they truly understand the personal price of leadership? The selection process cannot be taken lightly, for the student leaders will often determine the attitude, the atmosphere, and the level of achievement for the entire organization; they are the pace-setters for every member of the ensemble.

So many factors enter into this important choice. Are the candidates competent? Are they emotionally secure? Will they assume a leadership posture both in and out of the rehearsal environment? Can they handle stress and pressure? Are they willing to make decisions that are not self-serving but focused on their followers? Do they accept criticism and learn from their mistakes? Are they selfless rather than selfish? Ultimately, will they serve as positive role models for each and every band student? These are not easy questions to answer, but they are crucially important inquisitions, for it is unfair to everyone to assign leadership responsibilities to an individual who has not developed the level of maturity needed to assume the added responsibilities associated with productive leadership.

Over the years of teaching the skills and techniques of student leadership, I have observed so many students who are confident in their abilities and certain they can "do the job" and do it quite well; however, they have great difficulty turning hopes and visions into reality. The results are devastating to their followers, the program, and the perceived self-worth of the leader him/herself. In truth, everyone loses. How can we, as directors, avoid this dilemma?

In our urgency to have our students become more responsible and productive (perhaps these are one in the same), we are constantly looking for those opportunities of growth that will allow them to experience the pathway to success. After all, our fundamental mission as educators is to prepare students for the rigors of adulthood. It is exciting and personally gratifying when we see students rise to the occasion, but the penalty of failure has a high price tag in terms of the emotional damage to a student's self-concept. Unlike many other aspects of education, failure in student leadership means others are at the effect of the shortcoming. If a student leader does not accomplish the given task, it can (and often does) have a negative impact on all the followers, and the consequences can range from outward hostility to exclusion from the group. In extreme cases, the wounded student leaders will make a decision to never be put in a similar situation where they will be subject to such personal pain. They choose to sidestep any leadership responsibilities in the future.

Metaphorically, we do not pick a tomato from a garden until it is ripe, for it will be of no value to anyone. It is impossible to place the prematurely picked vegetable back on the mother-plant. Likewise, a student leader who is not ready (not ripe) will be incapable of surviving the pressure and stress of leadership if he/she has not grown to the necessary stage of leadership maturity. There is an art to the selection process, and veteran educators are careful to find the students who are:

- **Selfless** – Watch for the students who are always taking the time to help those around them. You can quickly identify this important trait—consideration for others—by simply observing their behavior before and after rehearsals.

- **Persistent** – Tenacity is an attribute necessary for attaining excellence at any discipline. Many people will begin a new endeavor with a sense of positive enthusiasm, but you are interested in the students who "complete" their assigned responsibilities. We are not measured by what we begin but by what we complete.

- **Consistent** – Most student leaders are at a time in their lives when they are establishing their personal habits and their life values; they are truly deciding "who they are." Dreams, goals, and desires can shift radically from one day to the next. Pinpoint the students who are predictable and demonstrate emotional stability; those who can "stay the course."

- **Affable** – It is often tempting to favor the student leader who is a gifted musician, and this is certainly an important aspect of his/her qualifications; however, it is vital for the student leader to have a healthy rapport with the other members of the organization. Popularity aside, the chosen student leader must be recognized and respected by the majority of the group.

- **Honest** – Slighting the truth is commonplace. The student who avoids the temptation to exaggerate or embellish the truth and is willing to accept the consequences that often accompany honesty is a rare commodity. Everyone will benefit from being in the presence of a person who demonstrates such personal integrity.

- **Faithful, Loyal** – "United we stand, divided we fall." This well-worn phrase is still classic advice for every leader. The students who are always tried-and-true loyalists are your best nominees for student leadership positions. At this stage of leadership, commitment to the group is mandatory, and any disagreements or issues should be dealt with behind closed doors and in strict confidentiality, but there must be a sense of unity in front of the ensemble members.

These six personality traits are only a starting point; however, they will establish a strong foundation for the selection/qualification of any student leader. We, as educators, must be sensitive to the overwhelming effects student leadership can have on the development of the individual. We are in a position to help our students create a sense of self-worth that will serve them throughout their lives. We can guide their efforts and energies to ensure a positive experience for all concerned. As their leaders, we have an immeasurable influence on their leadership for life.

A Paradigm Shift for Today's Leaders

The entire realm of leadership training has taken a dramatic shift over the last three decades. The strong-armed approach to leadership success has given way to the concept of allowing the follower to become an invested contributor to the overall mission. There is a greater emphasis on *intrinsic motivation* rather than using *extrinsic* rewards as a means to individual or group achievement.

The cornerstones of this paradigm shift emphasize a win-win concept embracing both the requirements of the project responsibilities and the welfare of the people involved. It diminishes the power struggle often associated with the traditional positioning, turf protection, rank-and-file status, etc. To find success in this modern-day blueprint of leadership style, these four laws of leadership must be understood and integrated into every decision made by the assigned leader; they serve as the foundation blocks of contemporary leadership.

People are more important than titles.

The focal point remains on the welfare of the people involved. The leader constantly monitors the overall attitude of the group, ensuring a sense of mutual understanding and synergistic effort based on individual and group commitment focused on the agreed objectives.

We can't lead others until we lead ourselves.

Role modeling plays a vital part in the leader's ongoing communication with the members of the organization. While delegation is still an important aspect of the process, the leader sets the pace by demonstrating the expectations and the standards desired to achieve positive results. The most effective form of leadership is positive role-modeling.

Leaders are measured by what they give.

Leadership is an opportunity "to give" to those who are part of the group, organization, ensemble. The position of leadership is a license to help all those who are part of the forum. If there is not a measured contribution to the forward progress of the group, the value of the leader is diminished to the point of being "merely a title carrier."

Leaders assume total responsibility.

When something goes awry, the leader immediately assumes the responsibility for the breakdown rather than pointing the finger of blame at anyone else. The welfare of the followers is primary in every facet of the leader's agenda.

Adapting this new leadership consciousness to any musical ensemble offers the individual players a greater opportunity to "own the group" and accept the responsibilities for the positive growth and development of the organization. Everyone wins.

The Personal Values of a Student Leader

When asked, "Who would like to serve in a leadership role as we continue to move forward with our band program?," do the students really comprehend the extended effort and energy required to fulfill the responsibility/agenda that lies ahead?

All too often an enthusiastic young want-to-be leader will eagerly assume the coveted title only to be quickly disillusioned following several unsuccessful attempts to garner group support while trying to accomplish the given project. Personal discouragement leads to "giving up," and (unfortunately) all future leadership opportunities are avoided based on past experiences of perceived failure.

Do we properly prepare our students for "what lies ahead" when they choose to become student leaders? Or do we simply (and randomly) pick this or that person to fill the given position? Are your leaders selected via a popularity vote, or are they chosen because of their abilities, skills, talents, and *intentions*?

Leadership is made up of two philosophical components:

1. Leadership is FOR GIVING.
2. Leadership is forgiving.

Many young people see a leadership position as the chance to be in charge, to tell others what to do, to delegate work, and to put themselves in a posture of authority. Nothing could be further from the truth. The essence of an effective leader lies in the student's ability to serve others, to create success for the people in the organization. It is the opportunity to give, to contribute, to roll up one's sleeves and begin moving in a positive forward direction. Whether it is straightening the chairs, putting the stands away, creating a colorful bulletin board, or working with someone on a musical passage, the leader is the person who does **what needs to be done, when it needs to be done, whether he/she wants to do it or not, without anybody asking.**

The second aspect of leadership centers on the concept of forgiving. When something goes awry (and it will), many young leaders want to react to the situation by reprimanding the followers for their inability to fulfill the leader's suggestions. However, the true leader will forgive the people involved and proactively refocus the energies to correct the problem and quickly get back on course. Psychologically (and intellectually) we know, "People do not get better by making them feel worse." All too often, there is a tendency for young leaders to chastise those who fall short of the given assignment; nothing could be more detrimental to the trust relationship necessary for future success in any leader/follower relationship. The solution is simple: forgive, correct, proceed forward.

When selecting those chosen students who will be working with their peers in a leadership capacity, look beyond their group popularity, their musical gifts, and even their academic standing; begin to observe how they interact with others, and pay special attention to those who always are considerate of their fellow students and willing to serve those by going above and beyond the call of duty. These are the candidates who are most likely to succeed as leaders; they "live" the values required of every contributing leader by *giving* and *forgiving*.

Choosing Leaders: Maturity Is the Key

- How do you choose your student leaders?
- Is there a specific criteria to use in the selection of these crucially important role models?
- Do you have a particular standard they must achieve before they are candidates?
- What are the expectations you have of these people?

After studying and working with countless student leaders over the years, it is clearly apparent: some students are ready for the extra responsibilities student leadership requires and many are not. What determines this crucial difference? It appears to lie in the area of individual maturity—not chronological age, but personal maturity. Some young folks easily assume (and consume) the added workload, while others may buckle under the pressure. As teachers, we have an obligation to be sensitive in our selection of student leaders, for we are asking these individuals to give up the privileges of their classmates and enter into a role that will demand their undivided attention if they are to succeed. As you can quickly see, being a student leader requires an individual to give up much of his/her freedom in return for the opportunity to dedicate more time and energy to the given goal.

While being a student leader is often misinterpreted as a status upgrade, it is, in truth, the acquisition of more responsibilities. It is all too easy for the aspiring student leader to be blinded by the enthusiasm of the moment and accept the charge before truly understanding what will be required of him/her. This is where we, as caring educators, must be cautious and realistic in our assessment of a student's "readiness." Once again, let us revisit the original questions pertaining to the selection process; it is imperative that we begin with this inquiry, "Is the student mature enough to emotionally embrace the task(s) at hand in a fashion that will positively add to his/her personal growth and development?" Simply put, "Can the student handle what will be asked of him/her?" Although there is no definitive template to measure something as arbitrary as maturity, there are some general guidelines that can help you in identifying those students who are being considered for student leadership positions.

Levels of Maturity:

Level I: Selfish – Selfishness focuses on the pre-occupation with "self." A student might be a stellar musician, but he/she easily becomes upset unless everything support his/her personal welfare and opinion. Beware of the student who unconsciously, or by design, makes decisions that supports his/her self-promotion and/or personal agenda. Little will be gained if he/she is given the power to make decisions that will impact others. Inevitably, more time will be spent dealing with the problems caused by immature decision-making than will be spent enjoying the benefits of the young leader's efforts. We often rationalize the fact that these students might, in fact, prosper by putting them "up front" or giving them extra responsibilities. Alas, it is rare they will rise to the occasion. It would be a much kinder and more positive choice to allow them to spend extra time in the growth process before asking them to put others' considerations and personal welfare ahead of their own.

Level II: Independent – We often see "independence" as a reaction to the lack of results achieved with a "selfish" attitude. The human mind comes up with a logical reason why others do not respond to our wishes and concludes, "It is easier to just do it myself than to depend on others and be disappointed." Many people function at this level throughout life and are quite successful; however, they are unto themselves and perfectly satisfied to "do their own thing." In fact, they may be uncomfortable letting others get involved. Since they produce excellence in their area of interest, we are often deluded into thinking they will transfer a similar standard of achievement to their followers if they are given a leadership position; however, the "independent" may become frustrated when the followers do not immediately choose to replicate his/her personal habits and work patterns. These individuals have a tendency to give up in disgust when the going gets rough and revert to the "I'll just do it myself" habit that has served them so well in the past.

Level III: Cooperative – A student must be at Maturity Level 3 (Cooperative) before being considered for any kind of leadership position that involves dealing with other people. Cooperative personalities are aware that nothing will be gained without a sense of mutual understanding and that all this must be well fueled with a cooperative attitude. Then, and only then, I–me syndrome gives way to a genuine we–us approach to every situation.

Satisfying the ego will become secondary to the forward motion and the personal welfare of the group. This student leader understands the benefits of cooperative decision-making are far greater than self-serving independent choices. Granted, it takes a mature individual to see beyond the instant gratification derived from serving oneself before thinking of others. Level III, cooperative, is a transition to the final and most important perspective needed for effective leadership.

Level IV: Giving – We have many examples of "givers," and we all know those who will go the extra mile, but this level of "giving" does not require any kind of reciprocation. Those who operate from a posture of "giving" do so for the pleasure of the process. The payoff for this individual lies totally in the opportunity to serve. While thank you's are appreciated, they are not required. The payment lies in the process of the giving. So often student leaders will find themselves discouraged because nobody recognizes their dedicated efforts. It is true we all enjoy personal acknowledgement along the pathway of life, but a mature leader is clearly aware that the most important affirmation of his/her leadership success is often disguised in the extension of more work and extra responsibilities being added to the leadership agenda. In essence, "The reward for a job well done is the opportunity to do more." The student leader who is a genuine "giver" is a rare commodity; everyone in the group will gain by experiencing the magic created by a *giving* leader. It is his/her *presence* that makes the difference; what greater role model could there possibly be for the followers?

The student leader selection process is certain to affect every aspect of your program. All too often we make our choices based on everything from age, talent level, attendance, personal favors, etc. In all fairness to everyone, we must be honest in assessing the maturity of those students who want to be given the opportunity to serve others through various student leadership positions. Carefully seek the student who wants to improve the conditions for his/her compatriots by unselfishly contributing to the given goal. When you find this individual you have identified a student leader in action. Put this individual in charge; let this student take the lead.

Solution-Driven Leaders: The Ultimate Choice

How many times have we heard the haunting phrase, "You are either part of the problem or you are part of the solution,"? In choosing our student leaders, it is vitally important to select exemplary role models who are *solution-oriented*, rather than *problem-plagued*.

Students who wish to serve in a leadership capacity must first understand that true leadership requires an individual to do more than his/her counterparts; it is about serving others. Student leaders are the doers, they are the people who roll up their sleeves and go to work.

Even after an extensive explanation of the personal and group expectations, I often wonder if the hopeful student leader really understands the level of commitment, dedication, patience, and personal sacrifice needed, required, even demanded. For those students who wish to take on the challenges of leadership, and for those directors who are looking for the student who has the right leadership qualifications, review the following thoughts, for these are the requisites in selecting and developing the solution-driven leader.

Focus on the solution, not the problem.

A gifted leader will seek an objective/solution and then begin to move in the direction of the given goal rather than dwelling on the current status and all the reasons the organization cannot reach the objective. This comes about by using a clear and concise blueprint of a *solution-driven* vs. a *problem-driven* plan of action.

The solution-driven leader (SDL) spotlights the strengths of the followers and emphasizes what is already working. Instead of quickly pointing out everything that is wrong, ineffective, inefficient, and preventing forward progress, the leader will first make a point to recognize the various aspects of the project (including the people) that give it credibility and make it worth the follower's investment of time and energy. The benefit package must be obvious, or there will be no ownership of responsibility by the followers and, thus, no group cooperation and lackluster participation.

The solution-driven leader sets a stage of open communication and personal involvement. Too often we look for those we can blame for the present predicaments; such behavior can garner initial agreement and emotional approval, but it has nothing to do with solving the problem. It is, at best, a momentary "feel good" and rarely serves the group or the leader. The SDL will create a safe, open forum of communication with everyone and begin to listen to any and all suggestions in an effort to attain a better outcome; in turn, everyone begins to become more involved in the implementation of a plan that reflects the group's thoughts and ideas.

The solution-driven leader keeps everyone focused on the goal. We often sabotage ourselves by dwelling on the opposite of what we want. Noted psychologist/philosopher, Abraham Maslow, said, "The mind will lead us in the direction of its dominant thought." If we spend our time thinking about why something will not work, we are leading ourselves to a predictable failure. A solution-driven leader will continue to communicate the desired goal to the members of the group; what the mind can conceive, the person can achieve. We must picture high-level achievement in our minds at all times and be realistic in the assessment of what it will take to reach the goal. This is one of the fundamental responsibilities of every SDL; focus the energy of the followers on the anticipated results.

The solution-driven leader creates energy and enthusiasm. The best way a leader can create energy and enthusiasm for a group is to model positive energy and sincere enthusiasm. This does not necessarily mean assuming the role of a cheerleader or extending shallow, ingenuine compliments. It merely means demonstrating a genuine care for the people, the goal, and the welfare of everyone involved. A lethargic, negative leader will drain energy from any group, and he/she will amplify the problems facing the organization; on the other hand, an enthusiastic, positive leader will infuse the group with the needed energy to move forward and discover the endless possibilities available as a result of group cooperation. The SDL understands the secret to all leadership, the one aspect over which he/she has complete control in every situation: *the ability to choose one's attitude at every moment of every day.*

The solution-driven leader creates an atmosphere conducive to effective and efficient problem-solving while giving continuous renewal to everyone involved. Being a leader does not mean "having all the answers." Young leaders often think they are responsible for every solution, answer, and resolution; such logic can result in frustration, confusion, and even delusion. A perceptive and effective SDL will encourage an ongoing exchange of helpful ideas from those who are part of the group. Every suggestion will be met with genuine appreciation, and the communication will be used as an opportunity to confirm the value of the person involved. (If we inadvertently or purposefully reject someone's suggestions, we stifle his/her creativity and create a barrier for further communication.) Maintaining an open, honest, safe environment for group problem-solving is seen by many as the most important contribution of any solution-driven leader.

Young people are often enamored by the "idea" of leadership and the personal benefits they perceive to be a part of the leadership position. Choose those who can comprehend the "reality" of leadership, those who are willing to go the extra mile on behalf of their peers, those who understand that the key to quality is determined by the collective work ethic of their followers.

I Went on a Search to Become a Leader

I went on a search to become a leader. I searched high and low.
I spoke with authority; people listened. But alas, there was one who
was wiser than I, and they followed that individual.

I sought to inspire confidence, but the crowd responded, "Why
should I trust you?" I postured, and I assumed that look of leadership
with a countenance that flowed with confidence and pride, but many
passed me by and never noticed my air of elegance.

I ran ahead of the others, pointed the way to new heights. I demonstrated that I knew the route to greatness. And then I looked back, and I was alone.
"What shall I do?" I queried. "I've tried hard and used all that I know." And I sat down and pondered long.

And then, I listened to the voices around me. And I heard what the group was trying to accomplish. I rolled up my sleeves and joined in the work.
As we worked, I asked, "Are we all together in what we want to do and how to get the job done?" And we thought together, and we fought together, and we struggled towards our goal.

I found myself encouraging the fainthearted. I sought ideas of those too shy to speak out. I taught those who had little skill. I praised those who worked hard. When out task was completed, one of the group turned to me and said, "This would not have been done but for your leadership."

At first, I said, "I didn't lead. I just worked like the rest." And then I understood, leadership is not a goal. It's a way to reaching a goal.

I lead best when I help others to go where we've decided to go. I lead best when I help others to use themselves creatively. I lead best when I forget about myself as leader and focus on my group...their needs and their goals.

To lead is to serve...to give...to achieve together.

—Anonymous
(as it should be...)

CHAPTER 5

Why Music?
Why Band?

Tim Lautzenheiser

After three decades of traveling across this nation and around the world visiting music rehearsal rooms, speaking at music conventions, presenting in-service workshops to music teachers, and enjoying the chance to work with our finest public and private school students, it is clear that today's young musicians have a distinct advantage over non-music students as they enthusiastically complete their elementary, middle, and high school careers at the top of their class roster and then predictably head full speed to their college of choice. They truly are destined to be "the leaders of tomorrow." Why?

- What gives these children an advantage?

- What do they have that non-music students don't have?

- Why are music students recruited with such intensity by every profession?

- Are *they* different or does learning music make them different?

We are on the cutting edge of breakthrough mind-research concerning "how the brain works." With the improvement of technology we can now watch the mind creating an endless (and infinite) network of dendrites (maps of learning) as the neurons continuously fire, establishing an ever-growing structure supporting the learning process. It is believed that music learning activates various areas of the brain and synchronizes the mind for learning at a fast pace while stretching the memory to a higher level of retention. Music enhances cognitive learning and facilitates growth in many areas of human development, i.e., motivation, social skills, time management, situational awareness, aesthetic appreciation, etc. As we learn more about the integration of emotional intelligence and cognitive learning patterns, it is ever apparent that the study of music has a direct relationship to the measured success of the individual student via reasoning, creative thinking, decision making, and problem solving.

The following chapter is dedicated to the non-musical benefits of music study; however, let me quickly add that the reason to *learn music* is to *make music*. Music touches a part of our psyche that helps us regulate our lives. Music helps us understand and express our moods and attitudes. Music helps us reorganize our thoughts and feelings while keeping us on track. Music allows us to respond appropriately in a social structure that is often confusing and complex. *There is no substitute for music for the sake of music.*

This chapter does not suggest the reason for music education is to bolster math grades or to increase SAT scores. However, it is clear that these are important educational benefits to parents who are making choices about their child's participation in music. The following pages are designed so you can share this compelling information with parents and decision makers. It will not make your band play more in tune or offer a suggested program of outstanding repertoire; however, it will open many eyes to convincing data in support of music for every child (the "musicians of tomorrow") as you introduce them to art and the joy of music making today.

Every child is an artist. The problem is how to remain an artist once we grow up.

—*Pablo Picasso (1881–1973)*

Why Music? Why Band?

Music for the sake of music. Any responsible music educator will emphatically echo this important mantra; it is the keystone theme that serves as the foundation of music teaching, music learning, and music performance. There is no substitute or replacement for music making as it relates to the positive growth and development of the human mind, body, and spirit. Participation in band avails the musician to the infinite journey of creative expression connecting to a language (music) that is understood, communicated, and appreciated by all of mankind around the globe. More important, music *is* a place for everyone.

Rightfully so, the emphasis of most music educators is the teaching of music. The young men and women who find their way to our rehearsal rooms are the focus of our daily teaching efforts and energies. The mission is to teach the mastery of musical skills so our students can access high-quality music and experience the joy of an ever-evolving sense of aesthetic expression. The intrinsic value of this musical blueprint is priceless, and every musician will attest to the immeasurable benefits of making music. Those who are a part of the musical culture adamantly agree on the importance of music; it *is* a fundamental need of life.

Granted, this philosophical perspective is very convincing, especially to those who have been involved in some aspect of music. In fact, it is inconceivable to musicians that music education is not considered a core subject in every school curriculum, for *every* child. Unfortunately this is *not* the case; therefore, if we want the students of today to become the music makers of tomorrow, the responsibility of "sharing the good news about the importance of arts education in our schools" must be embraced with a serious commitment accompanied by a diligent follow-through. We can no longer teach only the "interested students"; we must plant the seeds of interest and personally escort the students to the gateway of their musical futures.

Who Are Music Students?

- We know the majority (over 85%) of people who are musically literate *learn* music in the school setting, whether through general music classes, choir, orchestra, and/or band. It is apparent if students are not part of the school music program, there is little (if any) chance that they will seek to develop their musical skills outside the school setting.

- Many traditional recruitment programs do not offer multiple opportunities to "join the band." Although most music educators are eager and willing to accommodate any student who demonstrates an interest in being a part of the ensemble, the bulk of the students come into the program during the "beginner sign-up" event. One out of six possible candidates opts to become involved in band, orchestra, or choir. Shouldn't we ask ourselves: what about the other five?

- Over half of the students who enroll in a beginning music program during the middle school (junior high) years do not participate during their high school careers. For various reasons, they opt to drop their study of music within the first two years. Why? Are the parents privy to the negative effects this choice will have on their child's future?

- Most parents have little if any knowledge about the *positive benefits of music learning*. The compelling research generated over the last two decades has not (for the most part) made its way to the general public. While the music advocacy data is powerfully convincing, it certainly is not common knowledge.

Suffice it to say, there are many potential music students who, for one reason or another, have inadvertently missed the window of opportunity and, therefore, will (most likely) never have the chance to participate in a music ensemble.

Unlike teachers of other academic subjects, music educators must recruit (and retain) their students/musicians. With the evolution of everything from extended sports teams to advanced placement classes, the growing list of commitments before, after, and during school time amplifies the importance of choosing which organization(s) will become an integral part of the student's school culture. Such a decision must be approached with the knowledge and awareness of the impact it will have on the creation and nurturing of personal success habits of the individual. What stands to be gained as a result of the investment of time and energy? **Why music? Why band?**

Do parents (and students) understand the "indirect" benefits of music learning? Do we highlight character-building disciplines as part of the reason to be involved in band? Shouldn't we tout the fact that there is more to this music making than the intrinsic musical rewards? Unquestionably, *music for the sake of music* is primary, but can we afford to stop there? Many argue we could dilute the value of music education by focusing on the by-product rewards stemming from the group activity perspective: teamwork skills, self-discipline, healthy self-esteem, personal confidence, learning to reach short- and long-term goals, etc. This is a valid consideration, particularly from the educated/literate musician's standpoint. We know music itself *is* the driving force, the ultimate payoff; however, does this mean we should ignore the obvious data that quickly gets the attention of the non-musician parent? We cannot "teach young people musical skills" if they aren't in our rehearsal halls and music classrooms, so perhaps we would best serve *all* students by widening the spotlight of known life advantages enjoyed by musicians.

Parents must know there's far more to band than buying an instrument, taking private lessons, adding music classes to the school schedule, and rehearsing for a concert. Being a musician maps the human mind for success in all avenues of life. The learned skills needed to excel in music are transferable to every academic subject. Playing a musical instrument creates a multi-dimensional template of quality adaptable (and applicable) to every personal and professional challenge.

Through music learning we teach:

- An understanding of **quality** as well as the rewards of **quantity**.

- Behavior based on **ethics** as well as the importance of obeying the **rules**.

- Respect for **authority** as opposed to fear of **domination**.

- A working **wisdom** as well as a solid transcript of **achievement**.

- An ongoing development of **inner peace** as well as a workable plan for personal **security**.

Our educational system is heavily focused on assessment/testing. We measure the success and/or failure of the learning process through a series of evaluations. Clearly there has to be a scale to review, benchmark, and monitor the teaching process; it's the way we determine *learning*. All too often the numerical outcome becomes an end within itself, but it tells us very little about the pragmatic value of the class material. Shouldn't we be more concerned how this "subject matter" is relevant? We must ask: Can the "quantitative results" be integrated into the students' lives to promote better living, learning, and being?

Music, by nature, triggers both the cognitive and affective mind. Not only does the young artist experience the input of facts and figures, but he or she simultaneously develops an appreciation for art. We don't make music to get to the end of the musical composition; we make music to make music. The personal reward is not the final evaluation (as in a quantity-driven curriculum), but the intrinsic satisfaction generated as a result of *music making*. Music teaches an appreciation for *quality* as well as an understanding of *quantity*.

Ethics—Rules

For the survival of mankind and the perpetuation of our communal form of living, we must have rules to ensure the welfare of the community members. For the safety of the drivers on our highways, we have speed limit rules, and if these restrictions are not properly observed, a penalty is assigned to the violator. Society protects itself with guardians (law enforcement), spokespersons (attorneys), and interpreters (judges, juries) to guarantee we live in harmony while still enjoying freedom of choice. Although it would be altruistic, it is feasible there could be a society absent of rules if each individual believed, practiced, and lived an agreed code of ethics. In principle, the members of the group/community/band would be responsible for his/her behavior as it related to the welfare of the community/band; the responsibility for "harmony, balance, and blend" then falls on the shoulders of the individual rather than a policing agent. The choice for "doing what is right" is based on ethical understanding rather than the fear of admonishment.

The band culture (by design, by nature) requires each musician to behave in an ethical fashion. While there are certainly rules and regulations, the very fundamental structure of program excellence is based on the individual self-discipline contributed to achieve the group's goals. These are the character values we seek in every leadership role: band is shaping the lives of our "leaders of tomorrow" through the ethical habits they establish each day in the rehearsal setting.

Authority—Domination

We often muse about "the podium" being one of the last bastions of a unilateral leadership position. Yet we know a social order cannot move forward without efficient and effective decision-making. Band members quickly learn to focus on the band director's thoughts, instructions, and suggestions; the welfare/success of the band is (figuratively and literally) in the hands of the band director. Unlike many organizations in which a committee reviews every choice, the band world (accustomed to a fast-paced schedule of practices and performances) requires a leader/director who will make the call and move forward accordingly.

Band members do not have time to argue or discuss the band director's choice(s). Quite the contrary, they have learned to embrace and support the power of the authority figure and trust that the director's decisions will be in the best interest of the group. Healthy, happy societies are not solely based on the individual opinions of the members but on the mutual understanding of the importance of unity and the willingness to make personal sacrifices and contributions (time, effort, energy) to the agreed mission. The power base of the leader (the authority, the band director) is supported by the cooperative contributions of the followers (the band members). When the "respect for *authority*" overrides the "fear of *domination*," it establishes a positive atmosphere that opens the unlimited possibilities of the group's synergistic potential; it is virtually unlimited.

Domination, by intent, discourages creative thinking. The emphasis is on obedience (often "blind obedience") that supports the choices of the leader. As opposed to encouraging creative thinking, the environment of domination dictates "what to think" rather than "how to think." It rewards compliance (agreement and conformity) without the consideration for the welfare of the followers. Authority, on the other hand, encourages creative thinking while focusing on the importance of cooperation and the ability of the members to "agree to disagree" while still moving forward to sustain and promote the group's agenda.

Wisdom—Achievement

Our educational community continues to increase the testing component as an end-all for knowledge comprehension. The subtle implication is, "If it cannot be assessed, it not worthy of academic consideration." Of what value is all this rigorous data exchange if it is not applicable to the individual's life?

Now there is research indicating we can only remember and access the information we reinforce in our daily habits. Content (information) without context (an understanding of the benefits) is a dead-end street. The value of learning is not *what* we know, but *what we can do* with what we know.

Memorizing a long list of anything for the mere purpose of passing the test is an exercise in memorization, nothing more. Information recall is not the key to mastery; being able to see the *relevant value* of the information is the key, and it should be the focal point of the educational process. If we are only going to credit the value of higher test scores, we're doomed to live in a world of facts and figures. Certainly the quantitative aspect of learning is crucial, however, we should also be concerned about the qualitative value. Isn't this the very reason we choose to learn in the first place?

Being in the band deals with both achievement (a measurable set of disciplines and guidelines) and wisdom (learning that will support a positive, purposeful lifestyle). Band is one of the few areas of the school day that supports *expression* as well as *impression*. Music learning embraces all forms of cognitive learning and goes a step further by integrating the data into the human soul: EMOTION. Music reinforces the principles and ideals that have a significant and lasting effect on the way we choose to live. It teaches the ability to work with others, nourishes the love of learning, encourages cultural awareness, promotes cooperative flexibility in a communal climate, develops self-discipline, extends understanding, etc. All the while it *does have standards* and it *can be assessed*; there *are* testing evaluations that measure achievement, and there *is* solid evidence that the musical wisdom gained impacts the welfare of the learner. Simply put: Band makes better human beings and makes human beings better.

Inner Peace—Security

We humans continue along the pathway of *securing* various things to promote personal happiness. Whether it is a new car, a college education, a house, a boat, a job, a title, or any other extrinsic reward—the chase (and the race) for goal attainment is threaded into every aspect of the educational docket. When and where do we come to the point of personal satisfaction, the payoff, the joy of living life, and the very reason we choose to educate ourselves in the first place? Is success measured by *what we have* or *who we are?* Are we training students to focus on high test scores, or teaching students to enjoy a life filled with personal satisfaction? These are serious questions, for they determine the learner's mind-maps. Is the student connected to the *product* (the grade at the end of the semester) or the *process* (the holistic experience of blending intelligence, aesthetics, and emotion)? It's not about "just knowing the right answers." It's about "using the right answers" for what they can yield as a reference to meeting the challenges of daily living.

Every individual must determine his or her personal criteria for happiness. Nobody can (or should) dictate what brings pleasure and joy to the human spirit. Whether dealing with short-term goals or long-term goals, we often become so goal-driven that we ignore or simply don't recognize the importance of enjoying the journey as we attain our given goals; the very reason for *why we exist*. Band offers a new paradigm of learning. The music is the reason, it is the reward, it is the substance, it is the payoff. The means and the extremes are one in the same. We do not play music to get to the end of it; we play it to make music. In fact, if we are truly "connected to the process," we do not want the music to end, or the rehearsal to stop, or the concert to be finished. We acquire and develop a desire for expressing our inner thoughts and feelings through the music; we become artists and enjoy the highest form of personal satisfaction, *creative expression*, the fundamental component of self-satisfaction.

Why Education?

As the educational system continues to evolve, we often become so focused on the **how** that it is easy to lose sight of the **why**. Let us stand back and take a careful look at the development of the entire school system to gain a clearer perspective of not only *what* we are doing, but *why* we are doing it.

If the objective or purpose is to maximize the learning, we have to be boldly honest about what *learning* has lasting value and what *learning* is short-term and only for the sake of the test score. Are we more interested in producing students who are libraries of "commit-to-memory" information, or are we looking to develop well-adjusted students who are sensitive to those around them and interested in exploring their own human potential? Certainly there is a need for both of these avenues of educational focus; however, it seems we often sidestep the implementation of the learning in favor of *more learning*. The value of knowledge is measured by the fulfillment it brings to the knower. Is it worthwhile? Is it "worth my while"?

We have many high achievers (straight-A students) in our schools who have missed the mark in correlating their *knowledge* to personal happiness, social contributions, leadership skills, acceptance of others, desire to communicate with others, and ability to adapt to all facets of society. Is this the goal? Shouldn't our curriculums be designed to help the students open their hearts and minds to a life of ongoing *learning* while clearly demonstrating the benefits of critical thinking, integrity, dignity, compassion, honesty, ethics, responsibility, fairness, and creative expression?

If there is a shred of reasoning in the above thoughts, then the discourse **Why band? Why music?** takes on new meaning. We often tend to answer these questions from an artistic position:

- Music lifts our spirits.

- Music helps us share our inner thoughts and feelings with a vocabulary beyond the common word.

- Music avails us to emotions we otherwise will suppress or ignore.

- Music is a universal language.

- Music makes life worth living by bringing joy to our souls.

These are all well and good, and a resounding "AMEN!" is extended by this author; however, it is often difficult to express the importance of music making to someone who has never made music. The only way one can explain music is with music; it is a language unto itself. If we are to convince non-music makers about the importance of music learning, we may have to step off our podiums and put the *recruitment spotlight* on extended human needs and essential human qualities:

- Music has a direct impact on academic achievement.

- Music creates a forum for healthy human exchange.

- Music enhances perceptual motor skills.

- Music supports the qualities needed to survive and thrive in modern-day society.

Music is **not** a frill subject or a fringe activity, but music study is a microcosm of society bringing the requisite disciplines of success to the ensemble experience. Music learning for the sake of music; and music learning for the sake of life. What better way to prepare for a successful future?

Why Music? Why Band?
From the Non-Musician Point of View

Music is a place for everyone. Our traditional music programs have inadvertently promoted a false concept that "music is for the musically talented students." This elitist view has found its way to more people than we might expect. The study of music actually breaks down societal barriers from race to socioeconomic strata. Music often "reaches" the students who are struggling with their other academic studies. Advanced brain research continues to verify and confirm all brains are "wired for music." Eric Jensen, research author on brain-based learning, writes, "Music is part of our biological heritage and is hard-wired into our genes as a survival strategy." (Jensen, E. 2001. *Arts with the Brain in Mind*, p. 15)

Do parents, administrators, community leaders, and teachers of other disciplines understand (even know) this information? Are we (as music educators) sharing this extraordinary news with our educational partners? Music is not for the "chosen few," but music is for all those who want to pursue this exciting pathway of learning—and shouldn't that be everyone?

So many parents (at the point of registering a student for beginning band) do not understand the extended value of learning music. There's far more to this than investing in an instrument, scheduling lessons, driving to and from rehearsals, and/or attending concerts. The discipline of music making is transferable to every learning situation in and outside of the academic community. We have pointed to music students as "the smartest and most responsible students in the school." We now understand it is really the study of music that puts them in this favorable posture alongside their non-musical counterparts. We must be cautious not to suggest "music makes you smarter," but we certainly can point to the overall accomplishments of the students of music and find a similarly high level of achievement in both academic and non-academic arenas; this is not an accident or a coincidence. Arguably, no other discipline in school can better prepare the mind and spirit for the challenges of medical study, law school, classes in engineering, education/teaching, business college, etc. Ultimately, don't we want music to be a part of every person's life? From singing in the church choir to playing in the community band, music should not be relegated to the school environment. Music becomes our trusted friend of expression forever.

Framing the Message for the Welfare of the Child

What is the most important priority for all parents? *The future happiness of their child!* Mothers and fathers around the world dedicate their lives to creating an even better life for their children. In our highly competitive society, they want to see their sons and daughters have every possible advantage in their educational climate, their chosen profession, and their selected community of living where, once again, the cycle will repeat itself with and for the next generation. The complexity of society's evolutionary standards (some favorable, some not) puts responsible parents "on alert" at all times. What is the best use of their child's time and energy, both in the classroom and outside the classroom? Might I suggest the study of music is a cultural imperative fulfilling all the wants, needs, and wishes of every caring/sharing parent?

Instead of being overly cautious about emphasizing the "off the podium" benefits of music learning and music making, we might consider shouting this news to every accountable parent, to every administrator who seeks a better school environment, and to every student who wants to enjoy a life of happiness and success. This is not to replace or overshadow "music for the sake of music" but to reach out to all students so they can avail themselves to the rewards of music. We know we have the most convincing recruitment information available to bring them to our rehearsal rooms: *Music creates successful people.* The "learned outcome" of music study is a certain success blueprint. What parent could say "no" once he or she understands the immeasurable value of music study?

Why Music? Why Band?

It might be more appropriate to ask: **Why not music? Why not band?** It is evident music education should be experienced by every student. We, as a culture, will be best served if the hearts and minds of our youth are filled with the knowledge and the understanding of music. The time has come; the time is now.

CHAPTER 6

The One Who Makes a Difference: Characteristics of Master Teachers

Tim Lautzenheiser

Introduction

This chapter is focused on the makeup of the teacher, the conductor, the director, the maestro, the master, the mentor. There is much mystery about this critical component (i.e., the director) of the "teaching music" success story. Countless debates have been and will continue to be dedicated to these questions: Can we teach teachers how to teach? Do some just "have it" while others will never "get it"?

Perhaps we will never be able to come to a definitive agreement, and please do not assume such a complicated inquiry will be answered in the following pages. However, there are several characteristics worth our attention and our "attending."

We all know stories about gifted performers (the naturals) who sailed through every audition with ease, who could sight-read with remarkable proficiency, who were certain recipients of every conductor's praise, who seemingly never struggled with any musical challenge—and yet when it came to embracing the rigors of music teaching they found themselves struggling in the educational environment. What was missing? What went awry? Where did the system fall short? Why wasn't it working? All too often we simply shrug our shoulders and say, "Well he or she just didn't have the right stuff." However, that statement begs the question: "What is the right stuff?"

Why Do We Teach Music?

The reason we teach music is to connect the hearts and minds of our students to an expressive art form; there is no substitute for music making, music learning, music creating, and music listening/appreciation. Music itself is the reason for music. Although there are many extrinsic rewards and bonus by-products along the way, the intrinsic benefits cannot be duplicated in any other fashion.

Ask any skilled, serious musician why he or she participates in the process of making music, and the predictable answer will be a description of the priceless joy and intellectual stimulation garnered via the personal partnership with the music. If we take the query one step further and ask how they came to *know* the musical art form, the vast majority will credit this life-enhancing awareness to a music teacher, the person who planted the seed and consciously attended to the positive growth of the young musician. Clearly the relationship with *music* is the result (for many) of a caring-sharing educator who served as the *link* between the student and the unlimited possibilities of the language of music. That mentor is *the one who makes the difference*.

After thirty-plus years of traveling from coast to coast and border to border working with many of the finest band programs in the nation, it is apparent to me that there are some predictable attributes the finest band directors have in common. These master teachers are all dedicated to sharing their passion for great music with their students, their colleagues, their schools, and their communities. While they may have different pathways to achieving this goal, we can quickly see the common traits that serve as the cornerstones for their philosophical perspective and their personal approach to high-quality music education.

The Love of Music

Suffice it to say, the foundation of all master music teachers is a dedication to *music* and a commitment to introducing others to the personal understanding and enriched, extended landscape of creative thinking awaiting those on a musical pathway. Each of the following characteristics could be applied to the world of coaching, administration, management, etc., and they would be just as important. Do not infer that one could be a master music teacher by simply replicating the suggested character guidelines *without* the prime element of *music* being the focal point of every facet of the learning/teaching approach.

A Reality Check

As you read through the list keep in mind that it represents an overview of many who have dedicated their lives to the band directing world. While it would be wonderful for every bandmaster to bring all of these qualities to the rehearsal room, it is very unlikely, however, the maestro/master/mentor demonstrates an ongoing desire to raise the bar in all areas (both on and off the podium). We know that teaching perfection is as elusive as a flawless performance, but that does not deter the master teacher's desire and the will to achieve this intangible objective.

Let us explore these habits of success from the following points of view:

A. Musician/conductor
B. Teacher/director/administrator
C. Faculty community member
D. Personal pathway

1. A Purposeful and Workable Plan

Unless we know where we are going there is a pretty good chance we won't arrive.

The master teachers know their determined destination; they have a plan. It is easy to get entrapped in "the doing," and ignore "the planning." With so much "to do," daily activities become the driving force instead of the driving force (the plan) dictating the daily activities. The energies must be proactively dedicated to meeting the chosen goals instead of simply reacting to the various challenges of the day.

A. Musician/conductor:
- What repertoire will best serve the band?
- What will challenge the musicians and still be within their musical reach?
- What are the educational and artistic reasons for the program selections?
- What are the goals for this aspect of teaching music through performance in band?

Master teachers recognize the difference between playing through music and rehearsing the ensemble. Preparation (planning) time is as important as the valuable podium time. No time can be wasted with indecision or meandering, therefore planning is the conductor's primary job. Time on task is everything; lost time is simply not an option.

B. Teacher/director/administrator:
Is the schedule/calendar set? Is it realistic? Does it support the short-term and long-term goals? Is everyone aware of this information so proper energies can be devoted in support of these goals?

The commodity of *time* is often disregarded, forgotten, or overlooked. Yet time is the most important part of any plan, for it is the one commodity we cannot retain or regain. There is no time to waste (literally), and a purposeful plan is imperative.

C. Faculty/community member:

How does the plan impact all others in school society? Does it consider (for students) other activities and responsibilities? Are those who are connected to the program (administrators/colleagues) aware of the band's educational mission and prepared to support it accordingly? Can the school and the community connect to the band and feel a sense of enthusiastic pride?

We cannot stand alone, nor should we. The importance of outreach communication is beyond measure. While many will create a plan, that is only the first step; the plan must be distributed to all who are in some fashion attached to the band.

D. Personal pathway:

There has to be a balance *of* life and a balance *in* life, and the finest teachers are aware how critical this is if there is going to be a sense of professional satisfaction. Planning family time is a major component in the big picture. Planning personal growth opportunities (workshops, advanced degrees, quality musical experiences, etc.) feeds the soul on the evolving professional journey.

Teacher burnout is an all-too-common consequence of being a well-meaning and highly driven band director. With the best of intentions in mind, many have found themselves spent after a short tenure in music education. Those who are lifers will be quick to advise, "Take personal time to do something that will reset your mind, your attitude, and your perspective. Without proper rest and relaxation, you will burn up and burn out." Heed this tested wisdom!

2. Communication—The Foundation of Professional Success

The resolution to every problem will be discovered through sincere and open communication.

Communication is a learned skill; therefore, we can continue to improve our level of competency by dedicated practice. We must keep in mind that *communication success* is not based on what is transmitted, but what is received and understood. *Teacher presentation plus student comprehension equals learning achievement.* However, if the *teacher presentation* does not result in *student understanding*, then it becomes a futile educational exercise. Music *is* communication. Music *is* a language. Whether the communicator has a baton in hand or uses a verbal demonstration of a stylistic interpretation, the effectiveness of the process will be determined by that person.

A. Musician/conductor:

What is that special magic some conductors bring to the rehearsal or performance? Why do some directors instantly bond with the ensemble in a trusting journey of musical expression? Communication!

We have all witnessed the master maestro dramatically extend the musical terrain within a few short minutes: A higher level of player investment combined with podium leadership immediately enhances the imaginative artistic outcome. What *communication skills* have to be in place before this creative gateway is opened?

We must ask ourselves, "Have we established a *safe, challenging,* and *encouraging* environment that invites the musicians (students) to contribute, create, and communicate? Are we going beyond the notes on the page? Is there a benefit (for all) in connecting meaning to the music?"

B. Teacher/director/administrator:

Communication is the underpinning of every flourishing music program. People want to be in the know. In today's world of technology we can easily maintain a running dialogue with all those involved with the band, from the proposed rehearsal schedule for the week ahead to the registration deadline for the upcoming solo and ensemble event. Certainly there will be last-minute changes along the way, but we can minimize these with current, accurate, and assertive communication.

Communication often seems easier than it is, so when we are ineffective or run into any kind of barrier it is tempting to simply retreat and avoid any further confrontation. However, this creates another barrier, and we inadvertently set up a potentially more troublesome roadblock to understanding. Communication is much like intonation; we will be working on it forever, and it will never be perfect; but when it is ignored, things never improve.

C. Faculty/community member:

Communication with administrators, fellow faculty members, parents/boosters, community leaders, and, most importantly, students is primary. Problems occur when people are caught off guard; they often go into a reactive mode, causing undue angst on all fronts. When we can remove our own emotional perspectives, we often find that these situations can be avoided with timely communication. The mission of every committed educator is the ongoing healthy development of the students; in most cases, fellow teachers are eager to support a purposeful agenda, particularly when they feel the ideas or events are worthy of inclusion.

We will never arrive at consensus until we have a free and open exchange with all those who are part of our daily doings. We will never reach a satisfying conclusion until those around us are assured we have made a sincere attempt to hear their thoughts and concerns. While the final decision may not always be to their liking, the two-way communication invites input.

D. Personal pathway:

Communication with our fellow music educators is the network to our personal library of development. Communication with our families connects us to a support system that is absolutely necessary for a sense of well-being. The communication we enjoy in our spiritual lives will have a direct impact on our artistic possibilities.

There is no shortcut to success; excellence demands an investment of time and energy. If we are to maximize our input, we must embrace every avenue of communication available.

> I often ponder over the nature of true human sincerity. It is a rare and difficult thing; and how much of it depends on the person who is listening to us! There are those who pull down the barriers and make the way smooth; there are those who force the doors and enter our territory like invaders; there are those who barricade us in, shut us in upon ourselves, dig ditches, and throw up walls around us; there are those who set us out of tune and listen only to our false notes; there are those for whom we always remain strangers, speaking an unknown tongue. And when it is our turn to listen, which of these are we?
>
> —Anonymous

3. Teaching (and Being) with "Why" in Mind

...but WHY?

In an educational community that emphasizes assessment, it is easy to become entrapped in teaching the "what" rather than the "why." Although the assigned materials may be important requisites to the curriculum, the urgency to raise test scores and meet the administrative mandates becomes a higher priority than explaining the relevance of the data as it applies to the students' lives. As a result of this situation, we continue to add a vast amount of what to the minds of our young people, yet they are unaware of how or why it is important. Is this creditable learning, or is this merely an exercise in accumulating information for the sake of meeting the required minimum test scores?

With minimum communication skills, almost anyone can teach the what. High-quality educators will go the next step forward and demonstrate "how." The master teachers will base all exchanges on "why." The "why" is the key to creative thinking; it is the source of all intrinsic motivation. When "why" is part of the learning equation the student moves from a human *doing* to a human *being*.

A. Musician/conductor:

Is music the paper we put on the stand, or is it the outgrowth of how we interpret the dots on the page? Do young musicians understand *why* they are soaking reeds, oiling their valves, or tightening the bass drum heads? Are they simply going through the motions for the sake of teacher approval, or do they see the significance of their actions in relation to the benefits? Do we prepare the concert because "it's time for another concert," or do we use this opportunity to tap into the thoughts and feelings of the performers as they connect to the musical lines and explore a new level of expression?

From the first day of beginning band class, we have the opportunity to communicate our own enthusiasm for music making with the artists of tomorrow via master teaching:

- *What* needs to be done to meet the fundamental requirements of quality practice and performance?
- *How* do we develop these skills in the most efficient and effective manner?

And most importantly…

- *Why* is all of this essential in sourcing the unlimited talent within every individual?

B. Teacher/director/administrator:

For the most part, band is an elective class. Those who choose to be a part of band go above and beyond their other academic requirements. It is imperative that we communicate the importance of music education (the "why") to our new recruits and their parents, and that we continue to reinforce the "why" of music participation to insure the retention of veteran musicians.

Through newsletters, Web sites, and music advocacy data shared in concert announcements and program notes we can continue to educate our communities about the critical "why" of music in our schools. These efforts will bolster the status of music and break down false assumptions that music is reserved for only the talented, chosen few.

C. Faculty/community member:

Perhaps we will always be faced with the responsibility of justifying music in our schools. The music advocacy movement has captured the attention of decision makers as well as the general public. The "Why music?" inquiry is gaining momentum on all fronts. Regardless of our own opinions about "Why music," let us share our passion for music with everyone, particularly our teacher colleagues, those who are equally involved in preparing these young people for their futures.

Do our coworker associates know?—Music touches a part of our psyches that helps us regulate our lives. Music helps us understand and express our moods and attitudes. Music helps us reorganize our thoughts and feelings while keeping us on track. Music allows us to respond appropriately in social structures that are often confusing and complex.

D. Personal pathway:

We must take the time to step back and look at the "why" of our thoughts and actions. Boredom, frustration, and indifference are the results of becoming disconnected with the reasons we chose to be band directors in the first place.

Why do we dedicate our time, our intellectual energies, our creative talents, and ultimately our lives to the world of band directing? What is it about this musical, educational, organizational, administrative, always-challenging professional pathway that keeps bringing us back to the rehearsal room, to the performance stage, and to those extraordinary students who are willing to follow us with a sense of commitment unique to the school community? The answer is certainly different for each individual, but the common denominators are:

- The love of music
- The excitement of introducing others to the joy of music making
- The satisfaction of witnessing the growth of students as their talents unfold
- The chance to make a positive difference by connecting to the expressive language of music—creating art

4. Persistence Is the Key Ingredient to Goal Attainment

> Success consists of getting up just one more time than you fall.
> —Oliver Goldsmith

We are a culture that favors, anticipates, and even demands instant results. We want it, and we want it *right now*. Developing musical competence does not align itself with this contemporary theme; it requires perseverance, self-discipline, and a level of persistence foreign to many who have been weaned on microwaves and fast food. This does not suggest there is anything wrong with the huge strides we have made in "expediency," however, it does point to the fact that one must have a different mind-set when entering the world of music. There is no shortcut to achieving skillful dexterity on a clarinet, an oboe, or any of the instruments in the band family. Time spent on task is the one and only pathway to musical excellence. The master teachers inherently know that there is no shortcut and no substitute for dedication—practice, practice, and then more practice. (And when that is completed, even more practice.) This is not an easy sell for any educator, yet there is no place dedicated study and self-discipline is more obviously needed than in playing a musical instrument.

From a program standpoint, we also demand that time, effort, and energy be committed to extra rehearsals, out-of-school performances, and sectionals, not to mention back-to-school marching band camp, spring festivals, solo and ensemble events, and so forth. Without the fuel of *persistence*, a band life may be short-lived—for both students and teachers.

A. Musician/conductor:

A respected colleague once shared this professional point of view: "The easiest part of being a band director is the first day the band sight reads the music and the last time they play it on a concert. Our value to them is what we bring to the music between these two bookends, and, frankly, that is the best part of what we do." Perhaps this seems a bit simplistic, but it is certainly true. If there is not a measurable difference from the "first look" until the final performance, we have fallen far short. Every maestro/master/mentor eagerly anticipates the opportunity to enthusiastically dig into the score and lead the ensemble to new musical heights. We know this doesn't just happen, but is the predictable result of *persistence* combined with first-class literature and an insatiable appetite for musical excellence. This is a powerful recipe for success.

B. Teacher/director/administrator:

If there is ever a place where *persistence* is needed for the health and wealth of the band, the band community, the band family, and the positive future of the band program, the administration is it. We have all witnessed outstanding bands fade quickly when the leadership (directorship) shifts and the new leader does not dedicate proper time and energy to organizational and administrative responsibilities. Everything from proper grading procedures to financial accountability is an ongoing duty requiring constant attention. Too many potentially fine music teachers have been relieved of their duties because they neglected to take care of business. While it is certainly more aesthetically rewarding to rehearse the band, coach a sectional practice, or even give a private lesson, we must step back and view the additional assignment that serves as the lifeline for the well-being of the organization.

This popular bit of wisdom from the pen of President Calvin Coolidge serves as a forthright reminder of what it takes to make it to the summit of any metaphorical mountain:

> Nothing in the world can take the place of Persistence. Talent will not; nothing is more common than unsuccessful men with talent. Genius will not; unrewarded genius is almost a proverb. Education will not; the world is full of educated derelicts. Persistence and determination alone are omnipotent. The slogan "Press On" has solved and always will solve the problems of the human race.
>
> —Calvin Coolidge

C. Faculty/community member:

It is obvious that we can easily become disconnected from the rest of the faculty members, the administrative staff, and the majority of the students in the school setting. It is far more comfortable to reside in the music wing of the building and only venture to the main office when beckoned or have a student pick up our mail instead of greeting everyone along the way. Not being seen, heard, and/or recognized creates an invisible firewall of communication for all. The worst communication is no communication; we become conspicuous by our absence, and this is often interpreted as a lack of support or (much worse) a form of disengagement from the rest of the school. Granted, it is seemingly much more productive to work on the band library rather than make a pass through the teacher's lounge; however, the benefits of being an affable colleague are incalculable, and they will produce a bumper crop of dividends in the future. Although we may feel as though we cannot give up that time, the truth is we must be a part of the relationship building that is the outgrowth of these important dialogues.

The most common difficulties and personal upsets are caused by people problems. Building credibility with members of the school population is based on becoming genuinely interested and openly supportive of all areas of the school society.

D. Personal pathway:

When we envision those special educators we consider master mentors, these descriptive words come to mind: uncompromising, positive, relentless, unyielding, caring, passionate, and willful. They have "given up giving up"; their purpose is to serve, and they serve with purpose.

> The master asked his student, "How bad do you want to be good?"
>
> The student replied, "I want it more than anything in the world; please tell me the secret so I can realize my dreams."
>
> The master said, "Very well. You may have your wish. You already have everything you need; simply wrap it with the personal commitment not to quit until you've reached your goal."
>
> —Anonymous

> Until one is committed, there is hesitancy, the chance to draw back, always ineffectiveness. Concerning all acts of initiative (and creation), there is one elementary truth the ignorance of which kills countless ideas and splendid plans: that the moment one definitely commits oneself, then providence moves too. A whole stream of events issues from the decision, raising in one's favor all manner of unforeseen incidents, meetings, and material assistance, which no man could have dreamed would have come his way...Whatever you

can do or dream you can, begin it. Boldness has genius, power and magic in it. Begin it now.

—William Hutchinson Murray

5. The Exemplary Role Model Driven by Self-Knowledge

Know thyself. —Ancient Greek aphorism

It has been said we are the experts on one thing in life; and we know more about this topic than anyone else—and that topic is ourselves. It has also been noted a band program is a direct reflection of the band director. Combining these two themes is the final leg of our maestro/master/mentor journey. Being a band director may not be something we *do* as much as it is something we *are*. Improvement both on and off the podium will only become a reality when we choose to improve ourselves. Our students are mirrors of our own forward momentum; therefore, we must know our strengths and weaknesses and strategically work to promote the strengths and improve on our weaknesses. The master teacher is in every way the master student; the titles are one in the same: *the perpetual learner.*

A. Musician/conductor:

No one would argue against the importance of modeling great musicianship. If we slight our own musical growth it begins to reveal itself in the performance of the musicians in our ensembles. The decline is so incremental that we can deceive ourselves into thinking we are getting by. However, we are not, and our students suffer from this slow but very real downward musical spiral.

There is no replacement for listening to great music. With today's technological possibilities we can have the world's finest recordings tucked in our shirt pockets. Listening to gifted musicians performing extraordinary music is an artistic cleansing that replenishes our mission and raises our standards.

Make music. All those years spent diligently working on developing technical skills and musical awareness should not go by the wayside. We need to play music and our students need to see us playing music. Not only does it bring more beauty to our own lives, but it also keeps us closely connected to what we ask from our ensemble members.

Creation is the ultimate human motivation. We must listen to, play, and write music; it is vital to centering our life energies.

B. Teacher/director/administrator:

The old paradigm was: "Go to college and learn to be a teacher. When you graduate you will dedicate your life to sharing this learned knowledge with your students."

The new paradigm states: "Go to college to learn as much as you possibly can during your undergraduate tenure, and then start teaching and continue your educational growth throughout your career while dedicating your life to sharing your ever-growing library of knowledge with your students."

In the words of Winston Churchill: "I began my education at a very early age—in fact, right after I left college."

Unfortunately, many people view anything less than first place (or A+) as failure; therefore, there is a hesitancy to *risk*, to go beyond the comfort zone, to set our sights *too high* in fear of falling short, of *failing*. However we know success is a result of countless shortfalls experienced throughout the learning curve. Avoiding failure means giving up the opportunity for success. Ironically, we have to be willing to allow our students to witness our initial limitations followed by our commitment in action to overcome the challenges we face.

C. Faculty/community member:

Herein lies a critical aspect of any (and every) teacher's success, and it is often overlooked or ignored because we are insistent on having things our way. Carefully study the master teacher in action as he or she works with his or her colleagues and fellow educators. There is always an emphasis on cooperation rather than competition. We are part of the school community and it is vital that we exemplify harmony. This requires the wherewithal and the emotional maturity to *accept* the present status of every situation; rather than being concerned about "what isn't," we must begin to create "what it can be." Action takes precedence over reaction.

When the students (on all fronts) observe our willingness to support our colleagues and their programs, this becomes a life lesson plan in action. Infighting is always counterproductive, and polarization only thwarts the very goals (both musical and educational) we are trying to achieve: harmony, balance, blend, oneness, and ensemble. Should we not model what we are asking of students in both music and behavior?

D. Personal pathway:

While outstanding master teachers always recognize and acknowledge the positive achievements of students and supporters, they are never satisfied or complacent with the status quo; the goal of high-quality music education is constantly evolves as they reset the ever-increasing goals after each accomplishment.

Veteran teachers know that "the more you know, the more you know you don't know." Therefore, we must continue to refine our musical talents and skills while embracing the latest in the evolving world of technology; perpetuate the tried-and-true pillars of artistic growth while opening the mind to the latest tools designed to contribute to the efficacy of music education.

The mentor demonstrates a genuine love for his or her students, driven by a passion to share music with these impressionable young minds. The teachers who have a lasting impact on their students are those who exude a love of music combined with a heartfelt desire to enrich the lives of their learners.

Many years ago, I was listening to a clinic presentation by the internationally acclaimed horn virtuoso Phillip Farkas, who was then teaching at Indiana University after his remarkable tenure with the Chicago Symphony Orchestra. He was asked by a member of the audience what he thought was his most important contribution to the field of music. Without a moment's hesitation he said, "Oh that's easy; it's my students. All the recordings I have done are fine, but the real value of my work lies in the minds and hearts of my students, for they will be the ones to carry it to the next generation." There was a long silence in the room; his unassuming and genuinely humble opinion of his memorable performances was secondary to the importance of his teaching. He went on to say that he felt that teaching is the noblest profession in the world, for it is a selfless expression designed to make the world a better place.

Final Thoughts

The set of character attributes of master teachers is challenging, isn't it? To suggest all those who are master teachers model all of these quality traits would be absurd; however, we can begin to identify many of them when we describe our respected maestros, masters, and mentors. The point is that we can all strive to develop these enviable traits within the context of our own musical environments as a musician/conductor, teacher/director/administrator, and faculty/community member as well as along our personal pathways.

Our own lives have been guided by one or more mentors, those who went above and beyond the call of duty on our behalf. We are now in positions to return the priceless favor by being the stewards of possibility for those who enter our rehearsal rooms with a desire to become the music makers of tomorrow. They look to us for guidance, direction, advice, support, and encouragement. We stand in front of them as their maestros, their masters, and, for many, their mentors—the people who make a difference in their lives.

CHAPTER 7

The Cornerstones
for Program Success

Tim Lautzenheiser

Author's note

We all know there is no guaranteed "instant success" formula in the field of music education. Everyone has to go through a pathway of self-discovery, and it is often not an easy journey. Our colleges and universities continue to prepare some of the finest aspiring young artists, many of whom have indicated they want to commit their lives to the world of band, choir, or orchestra education. While some of these candidates do become lifetime members of the music world, far too many leave the teaching ranks after a very short tenure.

Why? After many personal interviews (with some of many of these one- or two-year veterans), it is apparent their choice to seek a new career had little to do with their love of music, but rather with their perceived sense of ineffectiveness in dealing with the overwhelming ""responsibilities off the podium.

In most cases, the beginning educator felt well prepared to embrace the rigors of "teaching music," and, in fact, pointed to this aspect of the teaching schedule as *the best part of the school day*. However, dealing with *all else* was simply more than they could bear…and, sadly, the passion for teaching music became secondary to vocational survival.

We have discovered there are many who have profited from a close association with a seasoned teacher who assumes the role of a mentor, guide, coach, trusted listener, loyal friend, etc. With this option at hand, the new teacher has a reliable source of information offering a tried-and-proven set of possible answers to a myriad of questions. Those who have been to the well have much valid advice to bring to the forum, and in many cases it has been the saving factor.

Please read the following thoughts knowing the data is derived from "observing" many of the finest master teachers in the profession. By no means will a bird's eye view of five select cornerstone success-components shift the course of anyone's teaching habits, but it can alert the reader to the opportunities possible in every musical teaching and learning environment.

By definition, a *cornerstone is:*

- something that is essential, indispensable, or basic
- the chief foundation on which something is constructed or developed

Introduction

Why do we teach music? It is one the first philosophical inquiries serving as an introductory question for every music education student, and it is also one we all must revisit time and time again. Countless books, essays, and research documents have been devoted to this important query, and, perhaps, our challenge is to recognize the collective value of all these important contributions. Through this process we then develop and create our own sense of purpose.

Simply put:

We are educating students in the realm of music literacy so they can connect to and tap the unlimited potential of their creative minds. Our educational goal is to teach the mastery of musical skills, so our students can access quality music and experience the joy of an ever-evolving sense of aesthetic expression.

There are certainly many spinoff benefits garnered by students involved in music learning and music making. By being in a first-class music program, they develop better organizational abilities, learn the value of teamwork, have the opportunity to test their leadership talents, and embellish many life skills that will serve them in every aspect of their personal and professional journey. These are *all* positive by-products generated via the music ensemble experience, However, they do not constitute the fundamental *why* of our efforts and energies.

We teach music because it is, unto itself, a standalone academic subject. Music touches a part of our psyche that helps us regulate our lives. Music helps us understand and express our moods and attitudes. Music helps us reorganize our thoughts and feelings while keeping us on track. Music allows us to respond appropriately in social structures that are often confusing and complex. Participation in music avails the musician of the infinite journey of creative expression, connecting to a language understood, communicated, and appreciated by all humankind around the globe. *Music for the sake of music.*

What role does the director, conductor, teacher, and/or mentor play in bringing this philosophical blueprint to fruition? Why do some programs thrive while others struggle to survive? Isn't it a combination of the message and the messenger? We all know the immeasurable value of the message; let us begin to investigate the key elements of the successful messenger. What have these master teachers (messengers) discovered, and what can we learn from studying and replicating their templates of success?

Observation

After four decades of working with some of the finest music programs in the world, it has become obvious there are marked likenesses that serve as part of the predictable framework of the successful band, choir, or orchestra program, and much of it is directly linked to directors and their approach to the art of teaching music. Above all, these people are dedicated students of musical growth; never arriving, always seeking, searching, and learning.

The following pages of this text reveal five off-the-podium cornerstone teaching areas that are found in many, perhaps most, of the outstanding music educators. While they all have a unique style, the following "cornerstones" are predictably evident in all.

Cornerstone 1: Continuing Education

I began my education at a very early age—in fact, right after I left college.
—Winston Churchill, 1874–1965

With modern technology and the ongoing exchange of breakthrough data, the educational process (school) is not something we do, but it is something we *continue to do* throughout our lives; it is never-ending, and is gaining momentum at warp speed.

Veteran educators are clearly aware "that the more we know, the more we know we don't know." Therefore it is necessary to constantly seek out the latest trends, techniques, discoveries, improvements, and educational benefits. It can be both exhilarating and exhausting, but it is a condition that is here to stay.

It is so easy and tempting to ignore the latest contributions, from the newest literature to technological breakthroughs. 'It is far easier to "do it the way we've always done it"—to not complicate the agenda with all this "new stuff" that really has not stood the test of time (often a convenient rationalization)—than it is to venture into the realm of the unknown. It is also much safer, but how can our students grow unless we grow? Shouldn't we be the role models of and for ongoing self-improvement?

Times are changing. Unlike days gone by, the teacher is no longer in a position of being THE all-knowing expert. Our students in many instances are more technological savvy than we are.

The Winston Churchill quote above is a wonderful bit of wisdom: we must heed the message within. "The completion of college requisites and the celebration of our graduation merely provides the gateway to the commencement—the commencing, beginning, or start—of our real education." Today's master teachers are also today's master students as they embrace the responsibilities of their awareness.

Cornerstone 2: The Value of Time

The one equalizing factor in this world is *time*. We all have twenty-four hours in the day—no more, no less. We can't bank it or save it, we either spend it or lose it. It's not a matter of "trying to get more time," but rather "managing the time" we have. What are the secrets to effective and efficient time management?

Make "Teacher-Only" Responsibilities a Prioirty

We often confuse "busy" with "productive." All too often we are busy, but we are not necessarily productive. It is easy to get caught in escape activities and, in turn, lose valuable time. It's important to focus on "teacher-only" tasks and develop a team of volunteers to take on other aspects of the work agenda.

Stuffing music folders, setting up chairs and stands, taking attendance, etc., can be accomplished by a select group of student leaders and/or officers. It is beneficial to take the time to teach someone else the "right way" to prepare music folders and the rehearsal room for the upcoming class. The rewards are twofold: students embrace more ownership of the ensemble's success, and the conductor/director is now free to spend his time learning the musical score along with other "teacher-only" duties (areas where the educator's expertise is wanted and needed).

All of this is so apparent, and yet from time to time, most of us find ourselves living in a sense of urgency because we do not have enough *time*. Why does this dilemma exist in the first place? The world of psychology suggests we subconsciously avoid more difficult responsibilities because:

1. *Doing less-challenging duties helps us avoid the disappointment we experience in unknown territory.* In other words, it is more comfortable and less taxing to stuff music folders and organize music stands than it is to analyze the thematic material of a new composition. We are not as likely to fail or feel as inadequate; it's an attempt to feed our sense of accomplishment, but the impact is short-lived. Avoidance is a human

condition; it is not that we do not know what to do, rather, we simply do not want to do it; in turn we look for opportunities that will divert our focus and still keep us busy.

2. *If we complete all the work there is to do, we might become dispensable;* we will not be needed. Therefore we must ensure we have a long list of responsibilities yet to accomplish. Subconsciously we really fear completion might jeopardize our perception of existence. Of course the irony is, the moment we finish one project, two new ones appear instantly. Every master teacher knows that the more we do, the more there is to do.

A review of these two conditions suggests we are effected by our own choices. If so, then we have the wherewithal to shift our emphasis and dedicate our time, effort, and energy to "teacher-only" obligations and duties so we can have a greater impact on our programs.

Acclaimed author and time-management consultant Stephen R. Covey offers several suggestions we can easily tailor to our teaching situations. The following checklist is an adaptation designed to accommodate the music educator in supporting a healthy program.

1. *What needs to be done right now?* What has to be accomplished immediately to meet a deadline and avoid a crisis situation?

2. *Does the task require personal attention or can it be assigned?* If it can be delegated to a responsible person, do so and move ahead to the next responsibility on the list.

3. *Is the energy being used within a personal sphere of influence to produce a positive result?* Beware of spinning your wheels; don't waste time if you don't sense forward motion.

4. *Is there an alternative way to create better results?* Avoid the "we've always done it this way" pattern of thinking.

5. *Does it feed the mission of excellence?* If not, do not do it.

No, this prioritizing template will not solve every problem, but it will clear up much of the confusion that prevents us from making logical choices concerning the investment of our time. It is also brings with it a tone of honesty so we are not tempted to fall into the all-too-familiar trap of *we don't have enough time.*

Avoid Communication Bottlnecks

In any ensemble class or rehearsal we must measure quantum time. If there are fifty people in the room and someone asks a question, the amount of time needed to respond (to complete the conversation) must be multiplied by fifty. For example: Two minutes devoted to a verbal exchange concerning a misprint in the second clarinet part is really one hundred minutes of used time. (Two minutes multiplied by fifty people equals one hundred minutes of "product potential.") This is not to say the problem should be ignored, but if it can be resolved outside the priceless ensemble time, it will be to everyone's advantage.

Establish a Culture of Excellence

From the moment young musicians walk into the room until the end of rehearsal, there should be a detailed plan for the most advantageous use of time. It is important to create, maintain, and support an attitude of positive learning through the establishment of a safe, challenging, and encouraging environment that reflects and respects the integrity of the musical art form. Unfortunately much time can be squandered because the expectation of excellence has not been properly explained (and reinforced) for the members of the organization. It is imperative we link self-discipline and group maturity to culture of the learning climate. (This is not to thwart the social aspect of the ensemble experience; however, rehearsal time *is* for rehearsal; 'use the time accordingly.)

Conerstone 3: Emphasizing the Why

The good teacher tells.
The excellent teacher explains and demonstrates.
The master teacher inspires.
—William Arthur Ward

Ward's words ring true in every aspect of our educational community; and perhaps they are most vivid in the world of music education. If we analyze the wisdom of his quote, we can apply it to our daily teaching habits and help us create a healthy atmosphere supporting the entire spectrum of music learning, music making, and music listening.

The Good Teacher Tells: The What

The very essence of educational process is "passing information from one source or mind (the teacher) to another source or mind (the student)." This represents the *what* in the curriculum. From "What year did Columbus land on the shores of America" to "What is wrong with the intonation in the low brass section," we are all trained to bring to our classrooms and rehearsals rooms a library of evolving valuable data (the *what*) to expand and improve the lives of our students. Even as we continue our own education via workshops, graduate school, seminars, conventions clinics, etc., we add to our own informational library. We know more *what*.

However, if all we do is *tell* our students this important data without holding them accountable for integrating it into their lives, we may be nothing more than yet another source of facts and figures. The overriding question is, "Is the material communicated in a way our students will realize it has a positive impact in relation to their well-being"? Rather, is it relevant to their lives, and does it have a lasting effect? Most certainly the *what* is a crucial foundation block, but we certainly cannot stop at this point in the process.

The Excellent Teacher Explains and Demonstrates: The How

This area of music education is one of the most exciting, since our discipline begs for explanation and demonstration. Successful music teachers know ""that hands-on learning processes are required for high-level achievement. We simply do not instruct *what* to do, but we show our students *how* to do it. We are participants as we sing, play, or explain by performing a phrase on a chosen instrument. Not only do we address the *how* of each vital skill, we *demonstrate* the tone we are seeking, the needed style, and the musical picture we are trying to paint. The class or rehearsal requires so much more than simply "telling students *what* to do"; it is a matter of discovering countless ways to *explain* the various avenues of efficiently and effectively reaching the given goal.

The Master Teacher Inspires: The Why

To inspire: to establish a creative atmosphere where the students are "in the spirit" of the moment and can express themselves in a way they far exceeds the *doing*, but begins to connect with the *feeling*. This is the *why* of learning. It is taking the *what*, combining it with the *how*, and venturing into a new realm of *why*. Master educators know when young musicians connect with *why*, they are making music; it is then that the motivation to strive for a higher level of proficiency takes on a whole new meaning. It triggers the intrinsic desire of the learner, and this opens the floodgates of expression for a lifetime.

As music educators we have a direct line to the inner emotions of our students. Much of the school day is "impressionistic" (i.e., learning the information and replicating it on a test). But music is "expressionistic." All members of the class or ensemble has the opportunity to bring their emotions to musical portrait; all have a unique value and play a key role in the creative process; all contribute their *spirit* to the musical community.

Unquestionably, any master teacher will use a combination of both intrinsic and extrinsic motivation techniques to bring student musicians to a higher level of technical proficiency, but—when all is said and done—the dominant motivation will come from the performers. It is their collective contribution that fuels the journey of musical excellence. The key to tapping the unlimited resource of human potential lies in the understanding of *why* we are being asked to do *what* we are being asked to do, and knowing *how* to accomplish the given task.

For Our Students

We must carefully explain the *why* so students can be empowered to contribute with the understanding of the personal and group benefits that will come from their invested efforts.

For Our Professional Welfare

We must take the time to step back and constantly look at the *why* of our thoughts and actions. Boredom, frustration, and burnout are the result of becoming disconnected with our reasons *why* we chose to be directors and conductors in the first place.

For Our Parents and Boosters

Do these great supporters *really* understand the lasting impression of music learning? Are they cognizant of the compelling data highlighting the extended benefits of music study? There is more to this than joining the band, buying an instrument, and attending concerts; far more. We have to make available to them *why* music is such a crucial aspect of the positive growth and development of every child.

For the Health of the Program

Let us be reminded we are privileged to be a part of an educational system that supports music education...and we get to teach it! Chosen musical standards determine how our students approach all situations they face, and when they understand *why* we set bar so high, they will also see the importance it plays in every facet of their lives.

What is about presenting information; *how* requires explanation and demonstration; *why* is the gateway to inspiration.

Cornerstone 4: Music for All: Sharing the Good News

How many people are aware of the following?

> Music learning activates various areas of the brain and synchronizes the mind for learning at a fast pace while stretching the memory to a higher level of retention. Music enhances cognitive learning and facilitates growth in many areas of mind development. As we learn more about the integration of emotional intelligence and cognitive learning patterns, it is ever apparent the study of music has a direct relationship to the measured success of the individual/student via reasoning, creative thinking, decision-making, and problem solving.

How many people should be aware of this information? We must bring this to the attention of everyone.

Like it or not, politics and education often go hand in hand. Since the school culture represents our most valuable natural commodity (children), it has a high priority on every political agenda. Veteren teachers know there is always a new and improved academic blueprint linked to every candidate's platform. From Back to the Basics to No Child Left Behind, each administration offers a new conceptual perspective certain to raise the level of learning for all students. The seasoned professional is often leery (and weary) of the latest slick phrase designed to attract the public's attention. In the ongoing commentary taking place in faculty lounges throughout our country there is an opportunity for us as music educators to establish a strong foothold highlighting the importance of music and arts education as it relates to positive development of the whole child.

Since administrators are being measured and evaluated on how well students score on various tests, school curriculums are being designed so every aspect of the learning process can be assessed in some fashion. While we can test, measure, and assess certain skills required for musical achievement, we are at a disadvantage when compared to a subject that is strictly cognitive in nature (i.e., math, history, English, etc.). If we are to justify the existence of music as part of the daily schedule, then we may have to expand our approach to include music advocacy. This is not to suggest we sidestep the obvious— music for the sake of music—but rather to expand the awareness of decision-makers: parents, administrators, colleagues, board of education members, community leaders, and (most importantly) the students themselves.

Since most of us were not trained to be music advocates, it is tempting to simply turn our backs on the ongoing discussions that will ultimately impact our music programs, our school culture, and society's future. If we do so, the fate of music programs is in the hands of those who are making decisions without a complete understanding that the value of music reaches far beyond the holiday concert or the spring festival. While these showcase performances are certainly a vital aspect of every musical organization, this is only the tip of the iceberg when we stand back and view the impact music learning brings to the entire educational forum.

The following information is compelling, and it needs to be given to those who are responsible for creating curricular mandates.

- Every child has the propensity to be a music-maker. Modern-day technology has allowed brain researchers to determine that music and art is part of our neurobiological system.

- All learning is enhanced via the development of musical mind-maps. Ongoing studies demonstrate the transfer of intellect from music to other areas of academic achievement.

- Music learning continues to be the most efficient and effective pathway to the development of important life skills, including problem solving, creativity, decision-making, and reasoning.

- The development of emotional intelligence is one of the strongest outcomes of music study. It prepares the student in the areas of social skills, self-discipline, time management, and aesthetic appreciation. Simply put, it teaches one how to be a sensitive and cooperative individual.

- Studying music develops thinking that encourages the exploration of the unknown, develops social harmony, requires alternative thinking habits, encourages multiple perspectives, and helps diminish survival prejudices. Successful music-making requires an emphasis on cooperation rather than competition.

In our efforts to avoid any contamination of our philosophical foundation, we may be prone to sidestep the indirect benefits of music study. However if we truly believe music is central to all learning, it is imperative that we not only embrace the latest data, but we tout it to those who will determine every facet of the school day from the hourly schedule to faculty assignments.

As stated, we are trained to be music teachers, not music advocates. While many colleges and universities are integrating music advocacy as a key component of various requisite classes, it is still foreign territory to most. However, if we, as music educators, are not the outspoken proponents for music education, who will be?

Cornerstone 5: The Master Teacher's Top Ten (or Everyday Wisdom for Being an Exemplary Role Model)

Pilots have a mandatory checklist they must go through before they are allowed to take off. It is designed to protect their lives and the lives of their passengers. Even the most seasoned flyers are required to walk through each of these requisites before leaving the ground. Perhaps it would be equally as effective if we, as music educators, had a similar checklist, a series of reminders to protect the lives of our musical passengers.

Know the Value of Personal Energy

Music is energy supported by aural motion. Whether it is the energy the teacher exudes from the podium, or the energy required to sustain a rigorous class schedule, meet performance demands, or take care of organizational obligations, the time-on-task for a music teacher is never-ending. We must face the fact the music teacher sets the pace for all students who are part of our ensembles and classes.

Express Appreciation

In every situation we are either appreciating or depreciating our environment, the given climate, and the atmosphere around us. When we appreciate a student, colleague, administrator, or parent, we lift ourselves as well as the recipient of the acknowledgement. In turn when we depreciate those around us with sarcasm or cynicism, we simultaneously chip away at our own self-confidence. Successful educators are quick to recognize and support individual and group growth, while also focusing on areas where improvement is wanted and needed. Musical success is an ever-changing combination of positive reinforcement (appreciation) strategically mixed with the never-ending quest for excellence.

Exemplify Optimism

Every student wants to be a member of a quality organization. Successful teachers always find victories throughout the process of learning. Since music is a language of expression, it affords the learner to feel as well as think. To be discouraging (removing the courage) may push the student away from the goal, whereas encouragement (creating the presence of courage) will oftentimes serve as the needed momentum for the student to embrace the challenges at hand. We certainly want avoid false praise (a shallow and dangerous tool), but we must always strive to establish an optimistic approach to tackling curricular objectives.

Avoid the Game of Comparison

We live in a competitive society, and—like it or not—we have auditions for chair placements, elections for officers, tryouts for solos, etc. Despite these built-in traditions, successful educators focus on intrinsic motivation (the opportunity to learn and to make great music) rather than extrinsic motivation (the chance to score higher than the neighboring school at a festival). If the goal is to reach a high level of musical performance, then the emphasis is on the process rather than the product. If the process is supported by the theme of quality music making, the product or outcome will reflect the investment.

Put People First

Taken directly from Stephen Covey's bestseller, *Seven Habits for Highly Successful People*, "Choose to understand before being understood." Each day we have budding young artists in front of us with one burning question in their inquisitive minds: "What will we do in music class or rehearsal today?" These special students chose to be in music because they want to play or sing; they want to express. When they sense we are confident about their abilities (as well as our own) and that we care for them as fellow musicians, the possibilities are limited only by the imagination.

Be Willing to Fail

This paradoxical concept is one of the masked secrets of successful people. We know failure is part of the pathway to outstanding achievement. Growth, in any aspect of life, requires risk-taking; one must enter the realm of the unknown and be willing to be disappointed while refusing to turn back until there is a sense of satisfaction that only comes from attaining a new understanding and a greater awareness of the possibilities at hand. To be in a state of creativity we must relinquish control and overcome fear. In essence, we must persevere in our ongoing climb to a new summit of quality regardless of the number of times we stumble and fall. Persistence is our most important companion in this quest.

Think Creatively

We live in a fast-paced society; our students are programmed to move quickly; therefore we must open our minds to new ways of thinking and being. If we do not, we are doomed to: remain the same: status quo, predictable, boring, simply going through the motions, stale. Rich rewards go to those who stand back and see the bigger picture, seek new opportunities, and look for ways to create artistic and emotional beauty within the learning environment. We must put meaning into everything by interpreting the present so it serves as a guide the future. This determines whether we flourish or flounder. Creative thinking can be the turning point in bringing new life to our programs.

Maintain a Healthy Sense of Humor

Unfortunately, many have linked "sense of humor" with "lack of substance." In the communication world, humor is the shortest distance between two people. Let's not confuse humor with flippancy, silliness or mere entertainment; humor is the way the human psyche creates emotional release. One of the traits of superior teaching is the ability to efficiently and effectively connect with students, and there are certainly times when a hearty laugh or an amusing tale will serve as the best teaching tool. And, above all, we must be able to laugh at ourselves. Teachers are humans, and humans make mistakes, so we must be willing to join in the laughter when we stub our toes. Then we can take a deep breath and get back to work. Humor is a lubricant of the mind and soul; keep smiling, and everything will run much smoother.

Demonstrate Professionalism

Self-improvement is ongoing, and true professionals are always striving yet never arriving, but continued growth is evident, and it is mirrored in and by ensemble members. Role modeling is arguably still one of the most effective forms of teaching. That being the case, we have much to offer through our dress, language, demeanor, and every aspect of our chosen behavior. Here is the opportunity to allow all contributing members of the group to witness the commitment and dedication we expect from them; it is the chance to "walk the talk," and do it with a sense of class and dignity.

Enjoy Teaching Music

Certainly everything on the daily to-do list is not always pleasurable or fun; much of it can be mundane and utilitarian. However, it seems like a small price to pay to have the opportunity to introduce a student to the priceless treasure of music. They cannot duplicate this knowing in any other facet of the educational community. There is no substitute for music; music itself is the reason to master the skills of music making. What greater gift could we possibly bring to young, impressionable minds? Music teachers do make a difference.

Conclusion

Cornerstone: a basic foundation block needed to support the framework of a structure or an ideology.

No doubt there are many key cornerstones supporting the successful music educator. Each of the five chosen for this essay has the wherewithal to be a separate study within itself; volumes could be devoted to a detailed exploration of any and/or all of these concepts. Hopefully the given ideas will initiate further thought, reading, and thinking, and—most importantly—some creative inclusion of these ideas.

In review:

Cornerstone 1: Continuing Education

We know the mind is not limited in its capacity to learn, and the more we bring to our knowing and knowledge, the more we can offer our students. Great teachers have a voracious appetite to continue along their own educational expedition.

Cornerstone 2: The Value of Time

The Declaration of Independence states: "We hold these truth to be self-evident, that all men are created equal...." Certainly one of the equalizing factors is time. It is not a question of, "Do we have enough time?" but rather, "What do we do with the time we have?"

Conerstone 3: Emphasizing the *Why*

Unless we truly can grasp the *why* of *what* we are doing, we may simply be "going through the motions." When we challenge our pedagogical lesson plans to clearly explain the *why*, the outcome of our teaching efforts is dramatically increased.

Cornerstone 4: Music for All: Sharing the Good News

Every human being is "wired to make music." The vast majority of music makers learned the language of music by being involved in a school music program. As we develop the language of musical understanding, we are also creating an archetype of mind capacity for other areas of curricular success. Music makes the difference.

Cornerstone 5: The Master Teacher's Top Ten
(or Everyday Wisdom for Being an Exemplary Role Model)

Everyday wisdoms suggests "a simple, easily understood" menu of ideas, and that is precisely what the fifth cornerstone offers. Wisdom is based on the knowledge of doing what is true or right coupled with good judgment as to the chosen action. The described top ten will serve as a dependable checklist for future success.

In the words of Albert Schweitzer:

> I don't know what your destiny will be but one thing I do know,
> the only ones among you who will be truly happy are those who have sought
> and found out how to serve

Strike up the Band...

CHAPTER 8

The Affective Domain of Band Directing: Developing Quality Habits of Highly Successful Music Educators

Tim Lautzenheiser

To the Reader

Please understand the following thoughts are laced with opinions based on four decades of being involved in the world of school bands. While there will be value in viewing and reviewing these suggestions, they are in no way to be considered *the* way, the *only* way, or even the *best* way to continue to fuel the journey to musical excellence. If the ideas are applicable to your situation and can bring heightened value to your students, use accordingly. If they do not resonate with your framework or teaching style, simply dismiss them as non-applicable.

The following nine mini-chapters are designed and written to stand on their own. Read them in no particular order; simply extract what will amplify the priceless value of music making for *you* and *your* students.

Mini-Chapters

1. Persistence: The Guaranteed Fuel for Success
2. The *Why* of it All
3. The Keys to Program Success
4. When the Teacher Is Ready the Students Will Appear
5. Requisites for Successful Teaching as a Musical Leader
6. The Realities of Recruitment and Retention
7. A Positive Attitude: The Key to Teacher Success

1. Persistence: The Guaranteed Fuel for Success

"The more we know, the more we know we don't know." It's paradoxical, isn't it? Perhaps this is the other side of "Ignorance is bliss." Those who are committed to *excellence* are always exploring new sources of information to increase their personal library of understanding. In doing so they discover uncharted horizons they could not previously even imagine. It is an exciting and endless journey.

As you read through this latest edition of *Teaching Music Through Performance in Band*, you are probably in hopes of finding some of the latest, most valuable data that will offer new possibilities for your own program. This is one of the predictable expectations we have of those people we have come to label as *master teachers*.

We are living in a time where there is a desire to *measure learning*. What determines *learning achievement?* Is successful learning based on test scores? From a musical standpoint is it:

- The results of the ratings and rankings of adjudicated performances?
- Pointing to professional achievement based on the number of participants in the given program?

What criteria do we use?

There are brilliant minds dedicated to the ongoing search for how we can objectively evaluate the learning process, and even they struggle to be definitive. Certainly there are no easy answers—as though there could or should be. However, while this intellectual discussion continues on many fronts, we *can* determine our own direction, our own methodology, and our own standards as we stand in front of our students each day. It is *here* where we can extend our learning, our knowing, and our growing to those young musicians who have chosen to be in our ensembles.

The truly great teachers embrace *what is* and move forward in the constant development of *what can be.* Certainly there are systemic mandates that challenge every educator, but they do not serve as a deterrent in reaching the given goal. The *master teachers* have given up giving up; they realize persistence alone is often the answer to reaching the destination. While it is easy to become discouraged or to lose enthusiasm, that simply is not an option for those teachers who are focused on reaching the chosen destination.

It is one thing to write about it, it is quite another thing to put it into action. One gains momentum by moving forward one step at a time. Whether it is inspiration, perspiration, or a combination of both, the willingness to *stay the course* is a cornerstone attribute of those very special teachers who walk-their-talk.

From Penny Kittle's delightful book, *The Greatest Catch: a Life of Teaching*:

When you're teaching you're going to see people who cut corners, don't work as hard as they should, or just complain all the time about everything. I believe you've got to do what's right, every single day of your life, even if the rest of the crowd isn't. Teaching is about honor and goodness and mercy. It really is. And no one will be watching you most of the time. You either live up to the calling of the profession or you don't, and most likely no one will ever know but you. But it matters because the kids are counting on you.

Therein lies the part we can control, our own daily approach to not only *what* we do, but the *way* we do *what* we do. Yes, we *do* have some say-so in all of this. We *do* have the wherewithal to take each present moment and make it a teaching moment. While our rehearsals and our classes might not reflect the perfect model, as long as there are students who choose to learn music and make music, we have work to do, and—as we know—it is some of the most important learning they will experience, and it will have a positive impact on every aspect of their lives. As Kittle writes, "But it matters because the kids are counting on you."

2. The Why of It All

Have you ever stopped to think *why* we do what we do? *Why* do we dedicate our time, our intellectual energies, our creative talents...ultimately, *our lives* to the world of band directing? What is it about this musical, educational, organizational, administrative, always-challenging professional pathway that keeps bringing us back to the rehearsal room, the performance stage, and to those extraordinary students who are willing to go the extra mile to follow us with a sense of commitment unique to the school community? The answer is certainly different for each individual, but the common denominators are the:

- love of music
- excitement of introducing others to the joy of music-making
- satisfaction of witnessing the growth of our students as their talents unfold
- opportunity to create a forum of learning to support the development of our future citizens
- chance to make a positive difference through the connection to the artistic world

...just to mention a few.

In many ways the above list is a reflection of the requisite assignment we all wrote for our Mus. Ed.101 class: "My Philosophy of Music Education." When was the last time we revisited those mantras? Is it possible we get so busy involved with the *what* of the doing we forget the *why* of the doing? In our urgency to responsibly prepare our ensembles for concerts, festivals, and contests, it is so easy to put more emphasis on the *extremes* (the goal) than we do on the *means* (the process), and in doing so we inadvertently sidestep the *why?*

So what? Why would it make any difference as long as the final outcome represents *a quality-based performance*? Who cares how we get there as long as we arrive? Won't the *why* become clear as soon as we accomplish the *what*? All are fair questions, and many would argue the *extremes* (the goal) justifies the *means* (the process).

From a different perspective, we know intrinsic motivation is triggered via the understanding of *why* we are doing this or that. Extrinsic motivation, on the other hand, requires something outside the individual to stimulate forward motion. Unquestionably, any master teacher will use a combination of both to bring student musicians to a high level of technical proficiency, but the dominant motivation will come from the performers. It is their collective contribution that fuels the journey of musical excellence: *not* the journey *to* musical excellence, but the journey *of* musical excellence. The key to tapping the unlimited resource of human potential lies in the understanding of *why* we are being asked to do *what* we are being asked to do. This is true for something as obvious as requesting a crescendo to an accompanimental phrase to support the musical line of the melody...or attending an additional rehearsal to accommodate a guest conductor's limited rehearsal time. When we comprehend the *why*, the *what* is much more easily accomplished.

There is more to this than joining-the-band, buying an instrument, and attending concerts...*far more*. We have to avail them to *why* music is such a crucial aspect of the positive growth and development of every child.

The band director is, without question, their most influential teacher. The standards you set determine how they will approach every aspect of their lives, and when they understand *why* you set bar *so high*, they also see the relevance of the same criteria as it applies to everything they do.

3. The Keys to Program Success

Until one is committed, there is hesitancy, the chance to draw back, always ineffectiveness. Concerning all acts of initiative and creation, there is one elementary truth the ignorance of which kills countless ideas and splendid plans: that the moment one definitely commits oneself, then providence moves too. All sorts of things occur to help one that would never otherwise have occurred. A whole stream of events issues from the decision, raising in one's favor all manner of unforeseen incidents, meetings and material assistance which no man could have dreamed would have come his way. Whatever you can do or dream you can, begin it. Boldness has genius, power and magic in it. Begin it now.

–Johann Wolfgang Von Goethe, 1749–1832
German poet, dramatist, and novelist

We all want to enjoy the benefits of professional success, and in our effort to arrive at this goal we often find ourselves constantly working to attain the level of proficiency required to be deemed *successful* by our colleagues, our supervisors, our students, our communities, etc. What are the requisites for success in the field of music education? Is it:

- Developing a balanced program in both performance, pedagogy, substantive curriculum, school pride, and community involvement?
- Receiving an invitation to perform in a national spotlight event with other stellar musical groups?
- Becoming the flagship of the community and being constantly recognized for outstanding musical achievements accompanied with public accolades?
- Having a large number of student musicians qualify for various honor groups?
- Developing many students who pursue music in their college life?

Do we really know the blueprint of music education success, or is this all a combination of opinions generated by others in our profession? Isn't the answer to each of the above questions a resounding *"Yes!"*? While we certainly have many guidelines to insure we are moving in a positive direction, there are many variations of the success/theme template.

Perhaps if we look at it from a different perspective we can understand more about this perplexing question by studying other successful directors—those who have traversed the pathway-of-excellence. Herein lies an important component we often overlook as we develop our own programs: What is it that makes this educator a resounding success? The answer, while complicated, appears to be rather simple:

- A command of the needed skills combined with an ongoing study for self-improvement. It is imperative we continue to refine our musical talents and skills while embracing the latest in the evolving world of technology.
- A relentless work ethic unknown in common hours. There truly is no shortcut to success. The "shortcut" is, in fact, the ongoing personal commitment to achieving quality in each and every aspect of our personal and professional lives.
- A genuine love for students and a passion to share music with these impressionable young minds. The teachers who have a lasting impact on their students are those who exude a love of music combined with a heartfelt desire to enrich the lives of their learners by bringing music to their lives.

- A giving spirit eager to convey the immeasurable benefits of music-making to everyone: students, parents, fellow faculty members, and *all*. The *master teachers* see everyone as a potential musician; their entire world is a classroom. Music education isn't something *they do*, it is something *they are*.
- A sense of inclusion and group ownership with countless ways to become involved at any level. Successful music educators open their perspective to see that music learning goes far beyond teaching notes and rhythms; it is about bringing people to music in whatever way is possible.
- A thankful and appreciative attitude linked with a developing visionary plan for program growth and development. While the outstanding music teachers always recognize and acknowledge the positive achievements of their students and supporters, they are never satisfied or complacent with the status quo; the goal of *quality music education* is fluid as they raise the bar with each accomplishment.

It would be easy to point to this recipe for success as a list of platitudes; let me suggest, however, that they are the cornerstone values that serve as the foundation for every *master teacher*. They are available to all of us; there is no mandatory degree or recommended preparatory curriculum, and the payment plan of personal investment will last a professional lifetime.

There is a somewhat of a paradox in all of this, and it comes from the notion that work means struggle, discomfort, extra effort, inconvenience, etc." enjoyment, being in the presence of *joy*, is usually the result of achieving or accomplishing a given task. We enjoy the victory of a job well done. We feel a sense of group pride and personal fulfillment following a great concert. We applaud our efforts at the conclusion of the performance. In many ways, *joy* is the final reward, however the successful teachers have learned to make the *process* as well as the *product* a joyful journey.

This does not suggest everything is all roses along the pathway; but rather than awaiting the final step to the summit, there are many acknowledgments of small successes along the way. Let us not confuse this with false praise or undeserved compliments; it is merely the recognition of forward progress. *Encouragement* (to offer *courage* to individuals) serves as the fuel to perpetuate positive momentum. Every rehearsal, meeting, lesson, or conversation is approached with a sense of purposeful possibilities as an opportunity for betterment.

Ultimately, our lives tend to mirror our individual thoughts and beliefs. Positive people live in positive worlds while negative people live in negative worlds, and—it's all the same world! We have a choice, and the outcome of our lives will be a reflection of the choices we make. As educators we know that our students, likewise, reflect and replicate our actions, habits, language, and attitudes; what an incredible responsibility we have. To this end, let us pledge ourselves to choosing excellence as the standard for everything we do, and *enjoy* the journey from beginning to end.

4. When the Teacher Is Ready the Students Will Appear

We continue to explore the various avenues of teacher preparation in hopes of finding the right combination to ensure a healthy learning experience for all students in their lifelong relationship with *music*. What *are* the attributes of a successful music educator? Do the students respond to *what* they are taught or *the way* they are taught? While the answer is *always yes*, we sometimes sidestep the contextual aspect of teaching methodology. Let us focus on the teacher as he or she relates to the students and discover that *When the teacher is ready the students will appear.*

1. Teaching Style: Positive or Negative

We would all like our students to evaluate us as *positive teachers*. It is important not to confuse the word *positive* with *happy*. By definition, positive means *honest and with forward motion*. There are certainly occasions when we are *positive* that things aren't moving in a *forward* motion, and the situation calls for some serious candor of an uncomfortable nature. Perhaps we can better understand the question by determining if we *enjoy* the process of teaching music. We must see it as an opportunity to bring our students to a higher level of creative understanding and expose them to a universal language certain to benefit every aspect of their lives.

Conversely, a *negative* style emphasizes reaching the given goal at all costs and justifying it by rationalizing. *The extreme justifies the means.* This often creates an environment filled with stress, tension, defensive and/or survival behavior, and (in most cases) it is counterproductive to what we are trying to achieve.

2. Motivation by Fear and/or Desire

Is it the fear of failure or the desire for success that motivates us to excellence? Is it the carrot out front or the whip on the back that moves the plow horse forward? It is clear we all are subject to both avenues of extrinsic behavior modification.

Fear is the quickest way to move or motivate (motor) a person forward. We are creatures of survival and, as pointed out, we will not be elevated to a higher level of behavior until we know our survival is ensured; therefore, any kind of threat will stimulate action in an attempt to preserve our very existence. The ever-popular and always effective, *"If you don't do this, I will..."* approach to students generates a quick response. From an outside perspective this appears to be the most efficient way to lead individuals or groups to the established goal. However, the after effects are usually not as desirable as we might hope they would be. If the student chooses to remain in the class or ensemble following a situation where *fear of failure* is the dominant motivational theme (many of them simply quit; the *path of least resistance* syndrome), then a behavior has been established that will require an even greater *fear* to achieve the next level of performance. It can be a one-way street to program destruction at the cost of creative artistry.

Alternatively, the *desire for success* does not guarantee such instant reactions. It requires a much longer and more patient style of mentoring. The sense of high-level accomplishment is often set aside in favor of rest and relaxation. Entropy is a not only a law of nature, but also a predictable human pattern. Ultimately we all want our students to study, practice, perform, etc., because of their innate love of music. This will only happen when the students *desire* to take on the responsibility with the understanding it has a personal benefit to their life.

Master educators use a healthy dose of *desire* and a judicious amount of *fear* as they traverse the endless musical journey with their students. Depending on the relationship that has been developed with the members of the class or ensemble, the application of these two extrinsic motivational tools is effectively administered at the appropriate time, resulting in a more-productive work ethic demonstrated by the students; herein lies the key to quality music education and performance.

The only true intrinsic motivation is self motivation; therefore our emphasis must always be the stimulation of the individual; to inspire the person so he or she will excel without being threatened or bribed.

3. Quieting the Ego

Is our quest for excellence in music a foundation of our teaching mission, or is it a payoff to feed our personal and professional growth pattern?

According to Webster's, *"The egocentric person is limited in outlook or concern to an individual activity or need."* Are we capable of rising above our individual needs to pursue a much higher goal? Can we give unconditionally without expecting or demanding anything in return? Can we get beyond our own *ego*?

These are uncomfortable inquiries, and, even as we ask ourselves, our ego will doubt the validity of the question itself. The I/me preoccupation with *self* is seen in every aspect of our society. The constant tug-of-war for ownership has not escaped our world of music. Students are sparring over chair placement, struggling to beat out someone else for a seat in the top group, jockeying for political favor to be the one selected as an officer, and on, and on. All too often receiving a *first place*, or being deemed "the best" becomes more important than making music.

Being number one becomes a higher priority than the benefit of playing, singing, and/or creating music. If so, the process alters accordingly to fit the goal. Students may walk off a festival stage thrilled with their performance, then discover they received a second-place rating which immediately throws the whole group in an emotional tailspin resulting in tears, accusations, blame, revenge, disappointment, and host of other negative reactions. If ensemble members felt a sense of positive accomplishment in preparing the music and dedicated their time and energy to achieving a new performance standard, then *why* would an evaluator's opinion override the joy of the accomplishment?

If the scenario above is true, the *extrinsic award* has become more important than the *intrinsic reward.* In truth, the rating is secondary. This is *not* to say there is not an educational value in competitive forums, but the evaluation or judgment *only* has educational worth when used to help prepare the next performance.

Outstanding educators detach themselves from the outcome. *The spotlight is always on the growth and development of the students,* which is the pathway of maturity.

4. Agree to Disagree: Harmony Is the Key

Harmony, balance, and *blend* are common terms in our rehearsal vocabulary. Are they also a part of our teaching pedagogy? Perhaps the solution to *quieting the ego* (point three above) is developing the ability to agree to disagree. The results that come from moving forward *in harmony* are generally far more beneficial than struggling with the handicaps of disagreement. It is certainly important to stand up for what we believe, but when it is at the expense of the overall welfare of the organization, we have the option to simply *agree to disagree.* It does not mean giving up our values, our standards, or our ethics; it simply means we support the dignity of the other party or parties and realize the discussion or argument is holding back the progression of the program.

Independently we rely on *energy:* "An individualistic source of natural power." Interdependently we avail ourselves of *synergy:* "A cooperative act such that the total effect is greater than the sum of the independent parts." This extensive boost in potential only shows up when we are in a cooperative mode. Rather than waiting (and wasting precious time) to find a group of people who are of like minds, we have the wherewithal to access *synergy* immediately (with any person) by agreeing to disagree, thus establishing a sense of cooperation—the key to creative synergy.

5. Our Mind Leads Us in the Direction of Our Most Dominant Thoughts

Thoughts lead to Feelings
Feelings lead to Actions
Actions lead to Habits
Habits establish Character
Character determines Destiny

This equation is an over-simplification of the programming of the mind. We take actions on our feelings; these feelings are a byproduct of our thoughts.

We have all been amused by our fellow music educator (?), Professor Harold Hill, center figure of Meredith Wilson's popular musical, *The Music Man*. As you likely remember Professor Hill was a capricious con artist who convinced the people of River City of the need for a band; this would prevent the innocent children from being lured to the evils of the local pool hall—a sinful establishment of ill morals!

In the story, Harold was finally confronted with his eager young musicians (instruments in hand) and challenged to make music or face the wrath of the skeptical town leaders who were rightfully suspect of the self-proclaimed maestro. He stood in front of the band to be with baton in hand and said, "Think!" Although it was a command of desperation, it was that very action that saved his hide, and it was—and is—a good lesson for all.

Whether we *think* we can or whether we *think* we can't, we're always correct.

It seems we often *wait* to see what the circumstances are, then adjust our attitude accordingly. However, the sequence is *believe* then *be*. With each passing hour we discover the power of thoughts and beliefs. The ability to manifest our desired conditions is known and practiced by every great teacher. The mind leads us in the direction of our most dominant thoughts.

What do you *believe* is possible for your students, your program, your school, your community? Are there *real* limits or are there only *perceived* limits? Are we held captive to our self imposed restrictions?

Any successful person will tell you there is more to this than simply thinking the right thoughts. The next step is to do the work necessary to complete the goal. It is not, by any stretch of the imagination, a quick fix, but it is a necessary beginning to achieve the aspired goal.

6. One Person Makes a Difference

YOU make a difference.

Every person makes a difference. We might want to ask ourselves, "What *kind* of difference am I making?" We are either part of the problem or part of the solution, but—without question—each of us makes a difference.

We often become frustrated because we feel as though we are alone in our quest. Our daily teaching schedule demands us to be a myriad of personalities ranging from a fundraiser to a bus driver, and somewhere in the midst of all of it, we teach music. The never-ending list of responsibilities can be overwhelming, and as stress and pressure are brought to bear, it is easy to retreat to the rationalization of, "I'm only one person and I can't make a difference." However, embracing such a notion violates the very goal for which we are striving.

Successful educators in any facet of teaching are the ones who see obstacles as opportunities for growth. They are not enticed by short-cut solutions, but are committed to reaching their goals and willing to invest whatever is necessary to achieve the given end. Styles vary, from those who are patiently methodical to those who enthusiastically lead the charge with trumpets blaring. The one commonality is *persistence—the ability to go on resolutely regardless of any inconvenience or opposition; to continue in spite of resistance.*

As we look through history it is evident the *only* thing that *has* made a difference is *one person.* Somewhere in our lives *one person,* probably a music teacher for many of us, was a catalyst in helping us choose our life's calling: *music.* Our teacher was *ready* when we *appeared.* Now we have the chance to return the favor; we can have a positive impact on the young people who eagerly step into our classrooms, for we know:

We make a living by what we get; we make a life by what we give.

—Winston Churchill

Requisites for Successful Teaching as a Music Leader

MANAGERS DO THINGS RIGHT. LEADERS DO RIGHT THINGS.

Many young people are enamored with the idea of being in charge, being the band director, being the musical leader. Our music environment lends itself to creating responsibilities that can be fulfilled by those who are willing to go the extra mile on behalf of the organization's forward progress.

Review (via your introspective filters) the following recognized patters of successful leaders:

- THE LEADER IS WILLING TO MAKER CHANGES
  Leadership requires challenging the status quo, questioning the-way-we've-always-done–it thinking, redoing what doesn't work, and improving what does work. By nature people are resistant to change; therefore the leader must counter such complacency by assuming the primary position of being the innovator of new and different strategies resulting in positive improvement for the organization or ensemble. Such actions do not always foster popularity; thus the leader must override the need for ongoing approval from followers. Through this process leaders take risks, knowing they will ultimately be held accountable for their actions.

- THE LEADER RESPECTS <u>ALL</u> THE PEOPLE
  Perhaps one of the most difficult aspects of being a leader is the necessity to respect everyone—not just those with whom we agree—*everyone.* Young leaders in particular often struggle when followers disagree or are unhappy about a decision. It is easy to react negatively instead of

proactively acknowledge those who offer a different perspective. When we are locked in disagreement, forward progress comes to a halt. It is imperative for the leader to rise above the antagonism of dissension to model and promote unity (even when all parties are not aligned in every thought and action), to show trust (although there may be divergent opinions), to promote pride (by demonstrating a willingness to include everyone), and to focus on the mission rather than spend energy being right about each and every aspect of the process.

- ### THE LEADER MODELS EXCELLENCE
  Leadership is not something we *do*, it is something we *are*. It is not something a person turns on and off, but it is a manifestation of quality disciplines that are integrated into each and every facet of life. Leadership is not a set of executed techniques that accommodate a particular situation; it is the outgrowth of a value system involving other people in an environment of fairness, honesty, and mutual respect. The leader demonstrates excellence by recognizing excellence in the contribution of others; the spotlight is solidly focused on the followers. The credible leader is one who epitomizes honesty, competence, positive visioning, and an inspired attitude. Leadership is not a part-time assignment; it is a full-time lifestyle.

- ### LEADERS ARE DEDICATED TO NON-JUDGMENTAL COMMUNICATION
  Leaders must understand the answer to every problem rests somewhere in communication, and in most cases, the most effective communication is *listening*. A leader promotes good communication by establishing a non-threatening atmosphere in which everyone feels free to share ideas without any concern for reprisal or embarrassment. The successful student leader avoids the typical make-wrong communication we typically associate with autocratic control. Instead, the best approach is one that encourages cooperation and supports the creative thinking of everyone in the group.

  These cornerstone character traits require a commitment to self development at the highest level. We cannot lead others until we lead ourselves; therefore self evaluation becomes a way of life. When the candidate leader understands and accepts such a challenging agenda, then (and only then) the foundation is in place to begin the exciting journey of leadership.

  We must encourage students to reach beyond their individual wants and needs, and in doing so, develop a level of maturity that will have a positive impact on the entire program. Our musical world offers countless opportunities for young people to test their leadership skills and talents at all levels of leadership responsibility. By explaining and emphasizing the four principles of quality leadership we can best prepare our student leaders for a future of leadership success.

When all is said and done, the best leader is and always will be the exemplary role model. Many can talk the talk, but the leader is the person who walks the talk.

The Realities Of Recruitment and Retention

Like it or not, recruiting and retention are the primary goals of every successful teacher, coach, band director, businessman, minister, etc. In any form of leadership, enrollment stands as the fundamental ongoing responsibility. Professional athletic teams hire entire staffs to scout for the best players, and then a second wave of people to convince these chosen ones to sign on and become a part of the organization. Outreach groups are constantly discovering new avenues of communication to bring more supporters into the fold. The world of advertisement and marketing would not exist if everyone simply ceased the game of involvement.

While many music educators seem somewhat hesitant to wave the banner of *music learning*, it is apparent the successful programs have a tried-and-true recruitment and retention blueprint that attracts new members and convinces present members to continue their participation; it is the lifeblood of any healthy band, a great orchestra, or an exemplary choir program.

Four Cornerstones of Recruitment and Retention Success

- Success Breeds Success. Music Learning Equals Success.
  There is no substitute for *excellence*. By design, the human creature wants to be a part of a quality group. While there are many tricks to the trade, nothing replaces the intrinsic motivation of young musicians who eagerly await their chance to be a part of *the best in the land*. The word is out when an ensemble represents the highest quality of musical artistry and appropriate behavior. *Music for the sake of music* is still (and always will be) the key component.

- Personalization.
  People join organizations when they are recognized for their potential and their value to the group. It takes far more than the "poster of invitation," that is merely the announcement of the chance to participate; recruiting requires special visits with new candidates, chats with parents, handwritten cards of appreciation, phone calls supporting inclusion of the student, and an ongoing agenda of outreach communication. Equally, retention of students requires a similar process. We often take for granted those

who tirelessly give their time and effort for the betterment of the group; there is much to be said for the value of *the spotlight of recognition*. Shine it brightly to include everyone, and shine it often. To assume all the students will re-up for the next year is a dangerous attitude; we need to extend our appreciation for what they have contributed and our enthusiasm for their wanted and needed leadership in the future.

- THE BEST RECRUITERS ARE THE PERFORMING STUDENTS.
  There is a reason marketers are quick to embrace the latest *hero* to be associated with their particular product; it suggests to the potential buyer, "If you use this product, you *too* can become a great basketball player, golfer, whatever." When the young ones witness their peers (of just a few years older) *enjoying* themselves in a performance, there is little more persuading to do. Let's not talk about the benefits of being in a musical organization, but let's allow the students to *experience* all the positive value by involving them in a specially designed *live performance,* and including the to-be musicians in some fashion will insure their desire to join the group. For effective retention, those students you invite to be the musical recruiters will become the loyal promoters of the organization. We all want to feel a sense of self worth, and it is up to you to provide this forum for them.

- COMMUNICATION: A THREE-STEP PROCESS.
  Step 1 Let the students you plan to recruit *know* how much you and the other members of the group want them to *join.*
  Step 2 Do an extended and personalized follow-up immediately after the recruiting effort.
  Step 3 Do a second follow-up a week later with another invitation to become part of the music family.

We are all good at step 1 of this communication process, but momentum is often lost on steps 2 and 3. In the sales world this is known as *the ask.* We must *ask* and *re-ask.* Many students are lost because we do not *ask* them (and their parents) to become involved in the program.

If we can focus on only one vital aspect of recruitment and retention success, it has to be *communication.* Those who emphasize the importance of personalized communication are certain to enjoy a healthy harvest of new musicians as well as a dedicated group of students who will stay the course and serve as key leaders for the continued growth and development of the program.

What a grand opportunity we have to connect young minds to an art form that will open their creative potential in every aspect of their lives. *Every child* deserves the chance to musically express himself or herself, and we have the chance to make it happen for them and with them.

A Positive Attitude: The Key to Teacher Success

What life means to us is determined not so much by what life brings to us as by the attitude we bring to life; not so much by what happens to us as by our reaction to what happens.

—Lewis Dunning

The word *attitude* often has a negative connotation. When we say a student has an attitude, it is generally interpreted as a description of a less-than-favorable disposition displayed by the individual in question. In truth, *everyone* has an attitude. Perhaps the key is to identify it with a descriptive adjective; a *healthy* attitude, a *positive* attitude, an *agreeable* attitude, etc.

We all want our students to display a *healthy, positive, and agreeable* attitude. Teacher stress (even teacher burn-out) is closely related to dealing with attitude problems. In most cases, we are properly prepared to teach the curricular information, but regrettably, an inordinate amount of time is spent dealing with other facets of the teaching agenda: student discipline, group focus, behavior problems, and classroom management, among others. In essence we are always working to upgrade group dynamics by dealing with students' attitudes. Developing students' skills and talents required to achieve *excellence* (in any facet of learning) is a result of creating a climate that provides a safe, challenging, and encouraging atmosphere.

So how do we go about making this happen? What are key ingredients needed to establish a positive learning climate? What can each of us do to contribute to the attainment of this educational goal?

Many people think the answer lies in systemic changes such as shifting the schedule, the classroom, the curriculum, the expectations, and so forth. While all of these can play an important role in establishing the ideal learning conditions, there is one area we know will have an immediate impact on the classroom/rehearsal-room setting: it is the *attitude* of the teacher.

In the words of noted author, educator, and philosopher Haim Ginnot:

I have come to the frightening conclusion that I am the decisive element in the classroom. It is my personal approach that creates the climate. It is my daily mood that makes the weather. As a teacher I possess a tremendous power to make a tool of torture or an instrument of inspiration. I can humiliate or humor, hurt or heal. In all situations, it is my response that decides whether a crisis will be escalated or de-escalated and a child humanized or de-humanized.

The collective attitude of students is, according to Ginnot, a reflection of the attitude of the teacher; that being the case, we can alter the classroom atmosphere by shifting our own approach, our demeanor, and our *attitude*.

A master teacher once shared the following bit of wisdom with me. It came at a particularly dismal time in a seemingly endless semester. I was fussing about the students, the administration, the parents, and even my colleagues. In my desperate plea for his guidance and help, this wise mentor asked me, "Do you want me to tell you what you want to hear, or do you want me to tell you the truth?" Of course I opted for the truth, not knowing what a painful yet powerful wake-up call he was about to deliver. He smiled and replied, "If you truly want to make a positive impact on the lives of your students, you must constantly ask yourself, *'If everyone in the class is just like me, what kind of group will it be?'* " The sting of his honesty jolted and bruised my ego, but it also offered a clear and concise solution to my self-inflicted plight. In other words, we cannot always control the various aspects of the educational system, but we *do* have control of our attitude; to that end, we have a tremendous influence on our students.

While there is no quick answer to maintaining a positive attitude, we can certainly integrate the following action plan to bolster our own approach to our teaching agenda.

- Develop a proactive response by embracing the notion of change.

    It is human nature to be skeptical (even cynical) about anything requiring a shift in habits. Avoid the pattern of instant reaction (often negative) by substituting a proactive perspective. Ask yourself, "What benefits can we garner by embracing the suggested changes?" The exercise of refocusing your mind on the positive possibilities will avoid the defensive reaction associated with any kind of change.

- Avoid conversations dwelling on the problems and shortcomings of the school environment.

    This is not to suggest we ignore some of the unpleasantries of the profession; however, we can sidestep conversations with a focus on negative commentary. Become solution-oriented rather than problem-oriented. Use problems as an opportunity to generate creative solutions. Choose to affiliate with the colleagues who are excited and passionate about their life's mission.

- Acknowledge those who are contributing in a positive, productive fashion.

It is easy to become consumed with identifying what is *wrong*; if we do not balance this practice by equally addressing what is *right*, our entire day can be spent surrounded by *wrong*. Unfortunately, we often let one or two personal rejections override a host of positive experiences. Maintain a healthy perspective by balancing the value of positive occurrences in relation to less-than-positive experiences. Many students, fellow teachers, parents, etc., are eager to express their enthusiasm and gratitude; be willing to graciously accept their gift of thanks and savor the moment. Put these appreciative folks at the center of your mental spotlight.

The key to developing a positive teacher attitude is not an easy task, for it requires a high level of personal discipline. It is far easier to simply point the finger of blame and conclude *nothing can be done*. However, such logic will be an idle servant for the teachers who truly care for the welfare of their students.

As Victor Hugo said, "There is one thing stronger than all the armies in the world, and that is an idea whose time has come."

Let us pledge ourselves to the idea of a positive teaching atmosphere supported by a positive approach to every aspect of our personal and professional lives; it is an *idea whose time has come*!

What you can see is limited by how far you look.
Your results are limited by your level of commitment.
Where you can go is limited by how far you care to reach.
Your level of achievement is limited only by the sum of your efforts.
The richness of your life is limited only by your imagination.
Your knowledge is limited only by what you're willing to learn.
Your experience is limited only by the things you choose to attempt.
The love you know is limited only by the love you give.
Your happiness is limited only by your attitude.
The person you can become is limited only by what you can dream.
The limits inside which you live are largely of your own making.
They bind or they vanish at your command.
You can hide inside them or you can grow beyond them.
The world is out there, waiting, any time you are ready.

–*Ralph Marston*

In conclusion, all of this data is merely a blueprint for *what can be.* After many years of observing master teachers in action. Within the template, the missing ingredient is the component of *personal taste.* We each must integrate our own perspective. While we can always replicate the methodology of our most-respected teachers and mentors, it still comes back to *being authentic* in our quest to connect our musicians to the immeasurable treasure of quality music making. With that said:

...STRIKE UP THE BAND...

CHAPTER 9

The Four Cornerstones of the Master Music Educator

Tim Lautzenheiser

- Role modeling a positive attitude
- Integrating a successful music advocacy blueprint
- Focusing on cooperation as the key to excellence
- Manifesting "the gift of giving"

When we examine the character attributes of the most successful educators, conductors, bandmasters, etc., we quickly realize they all reach a similar destination but via many different pathways. There are those who, time and time again, predictably create and manifest wonderful band/music programs within their schools and their communities and—more importantly—they achieve this goal regardless of the various circumstances concerning budget, facilities, staff, demographics, schedule, etc. What's their secret? What do they know and do that guarantees an environment of quality music learning and artistic music making? Is it *what* they do, or is it the *way* they do *what* they do? Or both?

The following sub-chapters address several of these non-musical (but closely related) aspects of the ever-changing world of music education:

- The keystone contextual concepts of master educators
- Telling and selling the value of music for everyone
- The artistic importance of cooperation in a competitive world
- The heart and soul of every exemplary music educator: the gift of teaching music

The Keystone Contextual Concepts of Master Educators

> When the National Science Foundation asked the breakthrough scientists what they felt was the most favorable factor in their education, the answer was: An intimate association with a great, inspiring teacher.

The above quote is attributed to Buckminster Fuller (1895–1983). Dr. Fuller was an American systems theorist, architect, engineer, author, designer, inventor, and futurist. American masters pay tribute to him as the most forward-thinking genius of modern times.

In the cognitive world of academic testing, measurements, etc., the above wisdom is not always recognized; rather, the emphasis is focused (for the most part) on cognitive learning...and yet, the proof is in the pudding. It is the teacher who is the key component to the success of the growing, learning, becoming equation.

This is not to sidestep the importance of the rigors of curriculum or data exchange—quite the contrary. However, it is to address the important link of taking the given information and integrating it into something that drives this world to be more civil, more appreciative, and more encouraging. It is *not* shallow self-appreciating, but digging in the depths of individual creative vision.

> He who has such little knowledge of human value as to seek happiness by changing anything but his disposition will waste his life in fruitless efforts and multiply the grief he proposes to remove.
> —Samuel Johnson

As music educators, what *is* our goal, our purpose, our vision, our "reason to do" and, ultimately, our "reason to be?" It's not about being better than someone; it's not about winning a huge number of awards, or monopolizing the first chair position time and again, but it is about creating the harmony of collective forward motion.

All else could well be a deception of sorts, and until we (as teachers and as role models) are charged with the responsibility of communicating the intrinsic value of music learning and music making in a language that resonates boldly with those who choose to be a part of our artistic environment, we are falling far short of the ultimate value of our professional (and even personal) contribution to the lives of our students.

> To believe in something, and not to live it, is dishonest.
> —Mohandas K. Gandhi
> (1869–1948)

CONTENT: What we teach.
CONTEXT: The way we teach what we teach.

By evaluating the components of our teaching contexts, we can adapt our roles as necessary and enhance our communication approach to maximize our invested efforts and energies and—above all—connect with our students so they understand the priceless value of the arts as a cornerstone of their tapestry of success.

What Is Our Teacher/Educator Personality?

Because we are "survival creatures," the fight-or-flight syndrome is always dominant in all behavior patterns. Dr. Abraham's classic "Hierarchy of Needs" suggests that the basic drive of the human is to perpetuate survival and, secondly, to defend our turf, whatever the given "turf" may be. When we threaten or attack another person, the response is generally a defensive stance or even an assertive posturing. With this knowledge, it is obvious why people are instinctively "on guard" and why they are hesitant to put themselves in any situation that is not perceived as safe.

As music educators, we must be keenly aware of the power of our words, for they serve as guideposts to our students. While one should never extend false praise, the notion of using any kind of fear-motivation (to put one in a state of peril) to encourage forward motion must be judiciously considered. The ultimate self-inquiry is, "Does the end justify the means?"

The age of "It's my way or the highway" may have come and gone. Master teachers are eager to trigger intrinsic motivation by focusing on the *why* of their instructional methodology. There are countless ways to offer the same message without demeaning the receiver of the message.

Attitude Development

The educational community has long emphasized the cognitive domain; this focus helps measure/assess *what* the students are learning. However, we know the affective domain can significantly enhance the learning process through self-motivation, creative thinking, visionary planning, and an enthusiastic approach to the rigors of learning, growing, becoming. To ignore the power of the contextual aspect of brain-based learning is to sidestep a key component to all higher-level achievement.

A willing mind is the gateway to all learning, and it is fueled by the accepting attitude of the learner. Simply adding more content is pointless unless the proper context (acceptance of the curriculum) is first established. Just how important is attitude? Reverend Charles Swindoll addresses the subject in this often-quoted insight:

The longer I live, the more I realize the impact of attitude on life. Attitude, to me, is more important than facts. It is more important than the past, than education, than money, than circumstances, than failures, than successes, than what other people think or say or do. It is more important than appearance, giftedness, or skill. It will make or break a company... a church...a home. The remarkable thing is we have a choice every day regarding the attitude we will embrace for that day. We cannot change our past...we cannot change the fact that people will act in a certain way. We cannot change the inevitable. The only thing we can do is play on the one string we have, and that is our attitude...I am convinced that life is 10 percent what happens to me and 90 percent how I react to it. And so it is with you...we are in charge of our attitudes.

A positive attitude is often misinterpreted as viewing the world through rose-colored glasses, being unrealistic, avoiding responsibility, sidestepping the difficult challenges, etc. In truth, it is just the opposite: a healthy attitude affords the opportunity to embrace the various challenges with a sense of optimism and hope fueled by a hopeful state of mind. It is driven by constructive thinking, expectations of success, personal persistence, inspired motivation, self-confidence, solution-oriented planning, and a willingness to reach the given goals. A positive (just like a negative) attitude is contagious, and it has extended implications to students, colleagues, and all.
William James, the father of modern-day psychology wrote:

> The greatest revolution of our generation is the discovery that human beings by changing their inner attitude of their minds can change the outer aspect of their lives.

Simply put, we are in charge of our attitudes, thus—in countless ways—we can determine so many facets of our professional (and personal) lives.

As a band director, the question is *not* can one person make a difference? The real question is: What kind of difference will one person make? To that end, the remainder of this chapter is focused on many of the off-the-podium approaches discovered in thriving music cultures, driven by master teachers who are keenly aware of their influence on each and every student who chooses to be a music maker.

Telling and Selling the Value of Music for Everyone

MUSIC ADVOCACY = PROGRAM SUCCESS

Author's note: Music advocacy is not, in itself, a particularly compelling subject. As music educators, we often feel burdened that we have to "justify" our existence in the curriculum of the day, and while we know it is critically important to the overall growth and development of every arts program, it certainly does not offer the same immediate gratification as a meaningful music rehearsal, or a great concert, a bountiful recruiting venture, etc. With that said, it is one of the most important pieces of the puzzle: it is the sleeping giant of every program, and once awakened, it *will* make a positive impact beyond compare. Be encouraged to embrace this mini-chapter with a perspective of the big picture, and the crucial role you play in embracing the significant role of being the shepherd of the arts in your school and your community.

The term "music advocacy" continues to be a key phrase for music educators throughout the county. Since the early 1990s, groundbreaking research continues to spotlight the importance of music education for *every* child. Everyone from civic leaders to political candidates has jumped on the arts bandwagon shouting (and touting) the benefits of music/arts education. It has certainly awakened the public, shifted the thinking of many school administrators, and created a long-overdue conversation about the educational, economical, and emotional value of music as it relates to enhancing mind development.

It seems ludicrous to "defend music in our schools." However, if we want our thoughts and beliefs to reach the decision-makers, we must "frame the outreach communication" using a vocabulary that highlights the value of music in their language, in their forum, and supporting their agenda.

Schools, by design, are created to prepare young people to assume the responsibilities of adulthood and become positive contributors to society— literally, to create a better world for their generation and generations to come. As our globe shrinks (via technology, travel, international relations, etc.), it is imperative that we understand and share our cultural differences in a peaceful fashion, creating a planet of mutual existence. Simply put, music is the universal language that enhances the awareness of others and supports the freedom of expressive differences; music encourages (even demands) creative visioning, critical thinking, self-expression, problem solving, risk taking, and it requires a high level of cooperation. Cooperation becomes the gateway to a higher level of aesthetic awareness and group achievement.

Music makes *the* difference. The discipline of music reaches many students who often struggle in other areas of school.

- Music is built on a platform that requires students to work together for a common goal.
- Music is a subject of self-discovery; the learning pattern is both impressionistic and expressionistic.
- Music is a place for everyone, from the most talented performer to the beginner; all levels of skill are accommodated in music class.
- Music crosses all socioeconomic borders; music is inclusive. Above all, it connects to the musician in a unique way, allowing the student/performer to witness and acknowledge his/her self-worth— yet another bridge to the understanding of one's unlimited potential.

Unfortunately, we often tend to sidestep the value of music learning as it relates to anything other than "music or the sake of music." However, if we are truly music advocates, let us embrace all growth benefits, especially when they are often the "common denominators of reason" to those who are creating, designing, and implementing the curricular blueprints for our schools.

In the words of Rolf Jensen, director of the Copenhagen Institute for Future Studies:

> We are in the twilight of a society based on data. As information and intelligence become the domain of computers, society will place a new value on the one human ability that cannot be automated: *emotion*.

We are in the business of "making better people, and making people better." While raising test scores is one means of accomplishing this goal, the experience of music making will afford students the opportunity to integrate the given data in a meaningful way that makes life worth living. With that theme in mind, let us pledge our efforts to the ongoing task of sharing the good news about the value of music for *every* child.

As we continue our evolutionary exploration along the educational pathway, the importance of music/arts in the school curriculum becomes ever apparent. In fact, it is no longer a convenient hypothesis based on personal experiences, but we have scientific proof: Music amplifies the human mental capacity (along with other identified benefits). Simply put, music is an essential element in the learning process. Neurological research evidences the positive impact of music study as it relates to the systemwide development of the mind's capacity and efficiency.

Music Is a Place for Everyone

As music teachers, we champion the theme, "Music for the sake of music." Let us never abandon this plea in defense of our artistic philosophies and goals; however, we must be wise and not turn our backs on the empirical research highlighting the multiple benefits of the arts (music); it is a discipline that fuels *all* areas of educational development. The study of music/arts links traditional learning styles to the creative possibilities of the human potential. Music can and does make the difference as it unleashes imagination—or, simply put, curious mind. It brings meaning to measurements and feelings to facts; it is worthwhile and worth our while.

Sharing the Information

Typically, we reach for the music research materials during a curriculum or scheduling crisis involving threatened staff cutbacks, loss of classes, or dropping various music programs within the school day. All too often, it is a last-minute attempt to salvage the music/arts program; usually it is too little, too late. We must tout the value of music learning every opportunity we have. We cannot start soon enough, and we must communicate the "good news" at all times—especially to those who need to hear the message loud and clear: administrators, parents, colleagues, civic leaders, and (above all) the music makers themselves, our students. The time for music advocacy is now...and always.

Here's What We Know

- Music making contributes to basic learning systems, including reasoning, creativity, cognitive thinking, decision making, and problem solving. This is the foundation/blueprint for success in every aspect of life.
- There is a measurable connection between music study and academic achievement. Those who are involved in music are at the top of their class standings within their given school. The effect of music study has an influence on mind mapping. Students can transfer to various disciplines within the school day and increase their productivity in every area of their educational landscape.
- Music serves as the catalyst in the creation of emotions, allowing the students to better understand themselves and relate to a world of complex social structure. Music students demonstrate a stability in their personal lives that helps them focus their efforts and energies on accomplishing their goals.

Music Learning: From Beginning to End

In the words of noted school author Eric Jensen, "The message with music education is: start early, make it mandatory, provide instruction, add choices, and support it throughout a child's education."

Who? What? When?

Who? We must laud the good news.

Music advocacy is a key component of every successful music program. As music educators, we have an ongoing responsibility to share the latest research findings with all those who are directly involved with scheduling, curriculum, academic choices, and administrative blueprints. We all have a vested interest in making certain every decision-maker is up to date on the important arts advocacy data that will have a direct impact on every child.

We must be able to articulate the value of music to the policymakers. With the constraints on every student's time, we are obliged to explain the incomparable value of music learning, both the direct benefits as well as the indirect brain development benefits; combined, they are building blocks of our *leaders of tomorrow*.

Unlike other areas of academia (math, science, history, etc.), music teachers are postured to ensure that music is offered as part of the curriculum docket. Whether this extra recruiting duty is right or wrong is not the issue; we simply must be proactive with parents administrators, students, and community leaders; it is a matter of standing up for what we know and believe.

What? Everyone must become aware of the fundamental importance of music at it relates to all of life learning.

Share the four basic music advocacy premises with those who determine the future of your program:

- Music learning is central to all learning. Music develops multiple brain systems; these learning patterns transfer to every area of the academic community. Music learning continues to be linked to high academic achievement. The correlation of the top test scores and musical studies is one of the key areas of neurological research.
- Music learning embellishes both cognitive and affective learning. From emotional expression to appreciation of diversity, music touches the human soul. When we analyze the assessment results of both affective and cognitive learning, the music students rest solidly at the front of the pack.
- Music learning enhances life skills. It contributes to reasoning, problem solving, thinking, creating, decision making—the tools needed to negotiate a successful life.
- Music learning continues to be linked to high academic achievement. The correlation of the top test scores and musical studies is one of the key areas of neurological research.

When is the best time to bring this information to the forefront? Now!!
We know most parents are not aware of the overall importance of the study of music or the way it maps the mind in all areas of understanding. They often see music class as an additional responsibility or an "add-on" to the regular class schedule rather than an academic cornerstone. Those who create the school mandates may not have access to this valuable information, nor will they unless we continue to bring it to their attention. With the increased emphasis on testing, assessment, higher standards in math and science, it is often convenient to overlook the significance of music in favor of a more rigorous focus on developing higher test scores. Ironically, the study of music is proven to support this goal as a by-product of the development of the creative arts mind.

The time is *now*. Music advocacy is no longer an option, but rather a necessity. We know it is a powerful message—that is *not* questionable. The question is, are we (as music educators) powerful messengers?

> Start by doing what's necessary, then what's possible, and suddenly you are doing the impossible.

—St. Francis of Assisi (1181–1226)

The Artistic Importance of Cooperation in a Competitive World

We are a society that thrives on competition. We compete in school for grades, we compete in our professional lives to achieve positions and titles, we compete in our daily life patterns for everything from a faster lane on the freeway to a winning number in the local lottery. We like to win, to get ahead, to maneuver ourselves to a better vantage point. Perhaps Darwin's proposed theory in his popular writing, *Survival of the Fittest*, clearly evidences our competitive spirit—our ongoing, ever-present striving to get to the front of the pack. It is powerful, motivational fuel for the human, but like any energy force, competition can be used in a positive and/or negative fashion.

The athletic community has very successfully embraced competition as a traditional outgrowth of the physical education curriculum. Football games, basketball tournaments, track and field meets, etc., have become mainstays of every institution. School themes are built around a string of victories or a state championship; the winning team often becomes the flagship of community pride. Though it is a gross generalization, we see winning as good, and not winning as not so good.

Observing the enthusiasm generated by competition, other disciplines have quickly jumped on the bandwagon. Our schools now have science fairs, 4-H shows, debate clubs, essay contests, and music festivals that recognize the achievements of an array of talents ranging from a flute solo to a 400-piece marching band. All of these organized competitive forums have created much excitement; however, we must be clearly aware that there can be a downside to the win-at-all-costs attitude. As responsible teachers, the cautionary responsibility rests directly on our shoulders. Take heed, for the instant gratification of first place can become a haunting detriment when it alone is the only measure of accomplishment.

When we ask students to "go the extra mile" by committing their valuable time to the art of making music, we must focus on the *intrinsic benefits* they will gain as a result of their investment rather than the *extrinsic rewards* that come as a by-product of their dedication. If "getting first place" is more important than the joy of an inspired performance (regardless of the outcome of the adjudication), then it is time to do some philosophical re-prioritizing. Is the goal to add more trophies of achievement to the shelves in the rehearsal room? Or is the goal to stretch the students to a new level of artistic communication? The musical growth of the students must stand as the top priority in every instance.

Over the years, the ongoing debate about the value of competition (in our musical world) has caused many music educators to avoid any aspect of adjudication/evaluation. Much like the ostrich with its head in the sand, this may be an over-reaction or escape; it may also be an unrealistic approach to preparing our students to address the realities of life. At the same time, if everything from chair placement to a solo audition is couched in a competitive framework, the need to overtake fellow musicians takes precedence over the personal growth and development gained by a solid practice program of healthy self-discipline. The key to a successful balance is achieved through the careful guidance of the teacher, the band director—*you*. Instead of dangling the proverbial competitive carrot in front of the students, we might be better served if we rewarded and recognized their success habits/patterns.

For example:

1. **Resolving a problem** – Many students are quick to recognize or identify problems, but there are few who will come up with a resolution. Those who do should be put in the spotlight and given responsibilities within the program.

2. **Being a quiet, innovative student leader** – Identify those silent few who are always finding ways to make things better. Discover the student who, without a hint of fanfare, is willing to help others and requires little or no personal attention for his/her efforts. This is a role model worth his/her weight in gold.

3. **Making decisions and taking action** – There are many who wait to be told what to do, and then they do it remarkably well. Look for those who go one step beyond and are willing to take a stand, make a choice, and follow through on their decisions; herein lies the leader of tomorrow.

4. **Loyalty** – In today's world, loyalty is a treasured attribute. Competition is the test of one's loyalty—not when we win, but when we lose. To avoid the "If we can't win, I quit!" attitude reinforces the character strength of loyalty. *Together we stand, divided we fall.*

5. **Cooperation** – Nothing is impossible when a group of individuals chooses to make cooperation the theme of their working atmosphere. Alternatively, it is almost impossible to move any group forward when they are constantly competing to gain the upper hand on their fellow performers.

It is apparent we need not beat another person (or persons) to win; we simply need to improve ourselves to experience the intrinsic victory that is a result of learning, growing, *becoming*. To this end, we must strive to support one another in the ongoing exploration of artistic expression and realize that the value of competition is merely a stepping stone for our students to witness others who share a similar passion. When all is said and done, we must *band together* if we ever hope to attain true victory.

The Heart and Soul of Every Exemplary Music Educator: The Gift of Teaching Music

Master teachers have always had the ability to "go beyond the assigned curriculum." Not only do they present the substantive requisite material in an effective and efficient style, but they also add a difficult-to-define bit of "magic" to the delivery. What *is* this secret ingredient that separates the exemplary educators from the rest of their colleagues? Many have attempted to quantify it, replicate it, diagnose it, and assess it in a way that it can be taught to others, and yet it seems (at best) very elusive. When we observe a master teacher in action, we know there is something very special about the way he/she "connects" with his/her students; it is far more than a "transfer of information." Rather, it is a complete exchange of knowledge designed to improve and enrich the lives of the listeners/students.

We tend to label this contextual gift with such terms as enthusiasm, expertise, people skills, communication competence, teacher readiness, proficiency, sensitivity, and even charisma. Yes, it is all of these—and more.

It is the right combination of personality attributes tailored to the given teacher, and it seems to be as individualized and as unique as the pattern of a snowflake. *Teacher magic* is an intangible.

We have all witnessed incredibly intelligent and well-trained educators fall short in a rehearsal or classroom situation. Likewise, we have observed an uneducated laborer captivate a group of students while explaining a particular procedure to accomplish the task at hand. Perhaps the *teacher magic* does not come from the extended study of a certain discipline, but rather, it is a manifested reflection of the values of the teacher. If this hypothesis is true, a master teacher could adapt his/her instructional skills to a multitude of learning areas. While it is arguable, an exemplary music educator could also be a winning coach, a remarkable youth minister could become a model teacher of foreign language, etc.

There have been many late-night discussions bantering the reasons why certain teachers enjoy ongoing success while others struggle to achieve a similar level of accomplishment. Undoubtedly, the controversy will continue forever; however, there may be a clue to the mystery in the following words of wisdom from the pen of popular Lebanese actor/comedian Danny Thomas:

> Success has nothing to do with what you gain in life
> or accomplish for yourself—it's what you do for others.

Therein lies the common denominator found in all master teachers: "what they do for others." As educators, we are measured by what we *give*, not by what we *have*.

As we continue our professional journey of teaching, rehearsing, sharing, *giving*, let us be reminded that the success of our programs, our ensembles, our students, and (yes) even our own careers is the outcome of "what we bring to others." Great teaching is not about the accumulation of various awards, trophies, and superior ratings; it is about creating a positive learning atmosphere for the students so they can understand, experience, and enjoy the language of music.

With this awareness at the forefront of our teaching philosophy...STRIKE UP THE BAND!

CHAPTER 10

It's About Time!
The What, How, and Why of
Student Leadership

Tim Lautzenheiser

The equalizer for everyone is *time*. We all have twenty-four hours a day; nobody has more or less. The success of our band programs is greatly based on how we use our *time*. It is rare to hear anyone in the profession say, "I don't know what to do with all this extra time!" In fact, it is usually quite the contrary: "I am running out time." If I only had some more time!"

While there is no way to s-t-r-e-t-c-h the clock, there are ways to prioritize the various responsibilities to make the best use of time in a positive fashion. What *is* the best use of your time?

1. Initially decide what is on your To-Do List only you can do, and put the chosen tasks at the top of the agenda. Examples include score study, communication with administrators/parents/community leaders/colleagues, making budgetary decisions, choosing repertoire, communicating with students about their contribution to the musical environment, serving as the leader in making decisions that impact the future direction of the program, being the musical go-to person, etc.

2. De-select the various time-consuming tasks that can be assigned to someone else, such as filing music, keeping the facilities in good condition, taking attendance, stuffing the folders, refreshing the bulletin board, taking inventory of fund-raising products, collating papers, putting up notices announcing upcoming concerts, etc.

So who does all this deselected work if it is not you? Who comes to the rescue to make sure the daily chores are handled while you (the director) invest time in preparing for the all-too-short rehearsals? Who can you *trust* to take on these various chores, knowing they play a critical role in the outcome of the group's success?

May I suggest it could well be the musicians who are the very heart and soul of your ensemble. Herein lies an unlimited source of human potential eager to become involved in the entire blueprint of *their* band program. They want to contribute, they can contribute, and they have the time...thus, it unleashes time for you to do what *only* you can do.

Whether you label these people student leaders, band staff, music aides, etc., it creates a new paradigm for the entire band culture and it postures you to truly be *the* musical guide as well as the program visionary; this is where your value is most wanted and needed.

It all sounds so simple, doesn't it? Just select a group of dedicated students, create a menu of responsibilities, describe your expectations, and then go on your way. Unfortunately, it requires far more than a mere, "Here's what you need to do, now go do it," assignment. Developing a team of first-class student leaders warrants an ongoing learning–growing–becoming communication from you. While it seems this endeavor only adds to your already overloaded work schedule, it is quite the opposite. Recall the adage, "Give a man a fish and you feed him for a day; teach a man to fish and you feed him for a lifetime." Metaphorically, we are "teaching our students how to fish." We are giving them the tools to think for themselves and discover the countless ways they can personally contribute and take ownership of the ongoing success of *their* band.

Having spent four decades helping develop student leaders, it has become ever apparent there are certain steps to be taken in the preparation and development of these wonderful hearts and minds. In addition to putting together a team of caring, sharing band assistants, you are also developing the leaders of tomorrow by creating the habits of success they can transfer to each and every aspect of their personal and professional lives.

Before jumping on the student leadership bandwagon, however, be aware of some of the pitfalls certain to be experienced:

- The student leaders' initial enthusiasm gives way to tedious and time-consuming work to be done; they simply give up.

- The student leaders fall short of the standards you have for your own work.

- The student leaders take on more than they can accomplish, and when they fail to meet their goals, frustration and disappointment set in.

- Time management is an ongoing challenge; the student leaders start too late and run out of time to complete the tasks.

- One has to extend constant reassurance to fuel the forward motion; a one-time communication doesn't have much lasting power.

- The work ethic gives way to teenage logic.

It would seem far easier to simply do it yourself and avoid all the potential conflicts. That way, you are assured everything will be done exactly the way you want it to be done! However, you have gone in a circle, and once again, you are using your valuable time in a less-than-wise fashion.

Student leadership is a never-ending journey of personal understanding. It's not a quick-fix formula, but rather it is a way of being, a style of thinking, a personal choice to go the extra mile on behalf of all those who are part of the band family. There is no absolute template of success, or magic potion, or fail-safe set of instructions that can or will guarantee the participating students will prove to be worthy contributing leaders. However, there are leadership skills that can be learned via a sequential curriculum designed to make the eager young candidates aware of what student leadership is all about.

The remaining pages in this chapter present the highlights of a twelve-week, step-by-step process designed to guide any willing student from, "I want to be a student leader," to "I know what I need to do and how I need to use my skills and talents in the advancement of our band program." The *Classic Leadership* curriculum certainly isn't foolproof; some will start and become disenchanted along the way, and they will simply give up. Others will struggle with how to integrate the newly learned leadership tenets into their daily habits. Of course, there will be those who quickly recognize they *can* make a worthy difference to their colleagues, the program and, above all, themselves.

Classic Leadership offers nothing new; there are no breakthrough insights. It is a road map, if followed carefully and faithfully, will bring about a newfound awareness of the immeasurable value of "serving others" for the advancement of all. It works when the student works. There is no shortcut to leadership success; it is a lifetime commitment certain to bring about personal benefits beyond measure.

For the complete copy of *Classic Leadership* (including the teacher's edition, student workbook, and accompanying DVD demonstrating the various leadership exercises) visit the GIA Publications website: http://www.giamusic.com/search_details.cfm?title_id=22936

For the reader:

The first chapter is printed in its entirety, including the exercises, the games, and the weekly assignment. Chapters 2 through 12 offer selected highlights from the chapters.

A preview video of a group of students participating in one of the exercises can be viewed at: https://www.youtube.com/watch?v=1DXjlBYTUVs

Chapter 1 Overview
So You Want to Be a Leader

The initial chapter focuses on the fundamentals of *servitude leadership*. It spotlights the key character attributes of the successful leader and offers the opportunity to create a leadership template to serve as a personal blueprint for all who choose to serve others.

"The value of a leader is directly proportional to the values of the leader."

The first step on your leadership journey.

There are two basic forms of leadership:

1. **Systemic Leadership**
   Based on officers and the traditional hierarchy of delegation

2. **Servitude Leadership**
   Focusing on the leader seeking various ways to support the followers and group by emphasis on ownership by all

Certainly there are hybrid versions of both. Neither is right or wrong, better or worse. They simply reflect a style chosen by the leader.

The following curriculum is dedicated in great part to Servitude/Servant Leadership. Be encouraged to stand back and look at the big picture when it comes to the challenges of leadership. It's certainly not all "glitz and glory"— it is often a most rigorous docket of responsibilities. Most importantly, it requires the maturity to see the world from a We/Us viewpoint. This is the fundamental key to all great leadership through history.

Case Study
Teacher: Use one of your own stories here that spotlights servitude leadership success.

The following article provides a clear starting gate for all aspiring leaders. Read it carefully and identify how it applies to your life and your future as a servant leader.

I Went on a Search to Become a Leader

I went on a search to become a leader.
I searched high and low.
I spoke with authority; people listened.
But alas, there was one who was wiser than I, and they followed
    that individual.
I sought to inspire confidence,
But the crowd responded, "Why should I trust you?"
I postured, and I assumed that look of leadership
With a countenance that flowed with confidence and pride,
But many passed me by and never noticed my air of elegance.
I ran ahead of the others, pointed the way to new heights.
I demonstrated that I knew the route to greatness. And then I
    looked back, and I was alone.
"What shall I do?" I queried.
"I've tried hard and used all that I know."
And I sat down and pondered long.
And then I listened to the voices around me.
And I heard what the group was trying to accomplish.
I rolled up my sleeves and joined in the work.
As we worked, I asked, "Are we all together in what we want
    to do and how to get the job done?"
And we thought together,
And we fought together,
And we struggled towards our goal.
I found myself encouraging the fainthearted.
I sought ideas of those too shy to speak out.
I taught those who had little skill.
I praised those who worked hard.
When our task was completed, one of the group turned to me
    and said,
"This would not have been done but for your leadership."
At first I said, "I didn't lead. I just worked like the rest."
And then I understood, leadership is not a goal.
It's a way to reaching a goal.
I lead best when I help others to go where we've decided to go.
I lead best when I help others to use themselves creatively.
I lead best when I forget about myself as leader and focus on
    my group…
Their needs and their goals.
To lead is to serve…to give…to achieve together.

—Anonymous (as it should be)

The Relationship This Has to Leadership
Leadership is made up of two philosophical components:

1. **Leadership is for giving.**
   The opportunity to create success for the people within the organization.

2. **Leadership is forgiving.**
   When things go awry, the leader "forgives" the error and moves forward.

Many people see a leadership position as the chance to be in charge, to tell others what to do, to delegate work, and to put themselves in a posture of authority. Nothing could be further from the truth.

The essence of leadership lies in the leader's ability to:
* serve others
* create success for the people in the organization

Leadership is the opportunity to:
* give
* contribute
* roll up your sleeves and begin moving in a positive, forward direction

Whether it is straightening chairs, emptying the trash, creating a colorful bulletin board, or working with someone on a personal problem, a leader is the person who responds to the tasks at hand.

A leader:
* does what needs to be done
* when it needs to be done
* whether or not he or she wants to do it
* without anyone asking

The next aspect of leadership centers on the concept of forgiving. When something goes wrong (and it will), many leaders often react to the situation by reprimanding the followers for their inability to fulfill their suggestions. However, a true leader will forgive the people involved and proactively refocus his or her energies to correct the problem and quickly get back on course. Psychologically (and intellectually) we know people do not get better when they are made to feel worse.

All too often, young leaders tend to chastise those who fall short on a given assignment. This can be more detrimental to the trusting relationship necessary for future success in any leader/follower relationship.

The solution is simple:
- Forgive
- Correct
- Proceed forward

Ask Yourself
- How do you see yourself contributing to this?
- How does it relate to you? Your life?
- Are you ready and willing to add these extra responsibilities to your schedule?
- Are you ready to make a positive difference?

Game/Exercise
1. Write down 5 character attributes you see as critical to being a successful leader. Consider the people *you* follow and what it is about them that garners your loyalty and support.
2. Discuss these positive attributes and then ask: How many would be willing to admit you **do not** emulate the character attributes you view as leadership cornerstones?
3. Next write down 5 character attributes you see as detrimental to the success of a leader. Again consider those who have been in leadership positions and have not achieved their desired results.
4. Discuss these negative attributes and then ask: How many of you would be willing to admit you often **do** demonstrate some of the attributes you find less than supportive of a healthy leadership personality?

What did you learn?
How is it relevant?

"Leadership isn't something you do;
leadership is something you are."

Assignment
What Do You Want the Organization to Achieve?

1. Make a list of 10 goals that serves as the perfect description of your "Dream Group."

2. The "Dream List" provides the framework or context within which an organization's strategies are formulated. Begin to create the foundation of a mission statement that will:

- guide the actions of the organization
- spell out its overall goal
- provide a path
- guide decision-making

3. The various group goals/dreams will serve as the blueprint to guide the focus of every action taken on behalf of the group's growth.

4. Write a letter stating why you want to be a leader and what you want to contribute to your organization/community via your leadership skills and talents. *NOTE: You will turn in this letter today for review at the end of the semester.*

Conclusion
 • Reflection

Homework...on your own
 Select a TED Talk (http://www.ted.com/talks) and/or article relevant to the development of leadership success to share with your fellow leaders.

Read the following article and align it with your own personality traits.

Character Traits of a Student Leader
by Tim Lautzenheiser

- Student leaders are no longer a luxury in our educational world, but rather a necessity. Any successful group is made up of a strong teacher/facilitator and a committed group of responsible and dedicated student leaders. We count on these extraordinary young people to offer their time and energy in the ongoing growth and development of our programs; without them, much of the daily work simply would not be completed.

- Students are usually eager to assume the leadership roles, but are they capable of assuming the additional challenges that accompany the real leadership agenda? Do they truly understand the personal price of leadership? The selection process cannot be taken lightly, for the student leaders often determine the attitude, atmosphere, and level of achievement for the entire organization. They are the pace-setters for every member of the group.

- So many factors enter into this important choice. Are the candidates competent? Are they emotionally secure? Will they assume a leadership posture both in and out of the classroom environment? Can they handle stress and pressure? Are they willing to make decisions that are not self-serving, but focused on their followers? Do they accept criticism and learn from their mistakes? Are they selfless rather than selfish? Ultimately, will they serve as positive role models for each and every member of the group? These are not easy questions to answer, but they are crucially important inquisitions, for it is unfair to everyone to assign leadership responsibilities to an individual who has not developed the level of maturity needed to assume the added responsibilities associated with productive leadership.

- Over the years of teaching the skills and techniques of student leadership, I have observed so many students who are confident in their abilities and certain they can "do the job" and do it quite well; however, they have great difficulty turning hopes and visions into reality. The results are devastating to their followers, the program, and the perceived self-worth of the leader. In truth, everyone loses.

- In our urgency to have our students become more responsible and productive (perhaps these are one and the same), we are constantly looking for those opportunities of growth that will allow them to experience the pathway to success. It is exciting and personally gratifying when we see them rise to the occasion, but the penalty of failure has a high price tag in terms of the emotional damage to the student's self-worth. Unlike many other aspects of education, failure in student leadership means others are at the effect of any shortcoming. If a student leader does not accomplish the given task, it can (and often does) have a negative impact on all the followers; and the consequences can range from outward hostility to exclusion from the group. In extreme cases, the wounded student leaders make a decision to never be put in a similar situation where they will be subject to such personal pain, and they choose to sidestep any leadership responsibilities in the future.

- Metaphorically, we do not pick a tomato from a garden until it is ripe for it will be of no value to anyone. It is impossible to place the prematurely picked vegetable back on the mother plant. Likewise, a student leader who is not ready (ripe) will be incapable of surviving the pressure and stress of leadership if he or she has not grown to the necessary stage of leadership maturity.

The following six personality traits are only a starting point, but they will certainly serve to give a positive format for all.

1. **SELFLESS**
   Selfless leaders are those who are always taking the time to help those around them. You can quickly identify this important trait—consideration for others—by simply observing their behavior before and after class.

2. **PERSISTENT**
   Tenacity is an attribute necessary for attaining excellence at any discipline. Many people will begin a new endeavor with a sense of positive enthusiasm, but you are interested in the students who complete their assigned responsibilities. We are not measured by what we begin, but rather we are measured by what we complete.

3. **CONSISTENT**
   Most student leaders are at a time in their lives when they are establishing their personal habits and their life values; they are truly deciding "who they are." Dreams, goals, and desires can shift radically from one day to the next. Pinpoint the student who is predictable and demonstrates emotional stability—those who can "stay the course."

4. **AFFABLE**
   It is often tempting to favor the student leader who is popular, and this is certainly an important aspect of his or her qualifications; however, it is vital for the student leader to have a healthy rapport with the other members of the organization. Popularity aside, the chosen student leader must be recognized and respected by the majority of the group.

5. **HONEST**
   Slighting the truth is commonplace. The student who avoids the temptation to exaggerate or embellish the truth and is willing to accept the consequences that often accompany honesty is a rare commodity. Everyone will benefit from being in the presence of a person who demonstrates such personal integrity.

6. **FAITHFUL, LOYAL**

   "United we stand, divided we fall." This well-worn phrase is still classic advice for every leader. The students who are always tried-and-true loyalists are your best nominees for student leadership positions. At this stage of leadership, commitment to the group is mandatory, and any disagreements or issues should be dealt with behind closed doors and in strict confidentiality, but there must be a sense of unity in front of the group members.

Chapter 2 Overview
Create a Mission Statement

It is critical for the all the leaders to agree on the direction of their given efforts and energies. The mission statement represents the essence of the *why* of the group's purpose. Everyone must embrace the mission statement and what it stands for.

The mission statement should:

- guide the actions of the organization
- spell out its overall goal
- provide a path
- influence all decision-making

The mission statement provides the framework or context within which the organization's strategies are formulated. While it is often a tedious exercise, it guarantees there is an agreement concerning the WHY of the mission, it will help design HOW to achieve the given goals, so you can begin doing WHAT needs to be done.

The Relationship This Has to Leadership

We are all subject to the deceptive trap of leadership. It is easy to become excited about the platitudes and forget the importance (and necessity) of doing the work that is:

- pragmatic
- measurable
- relative
- supportive of the mission statement

Leaders who are firmly grounded will dedicate time and energy to contributing in a fashion that is clearly making a difference in promoting the declared mission statement.

Now: define the agreed-upon mission statement and put it in writing.

Chapter 3 Overview
Creative Goal Setting

"We can't arrive at the destination unless we know where we are going." The goal-setting process gives everyone the chance to contribute in positive fashion to attain the agreed-upon goals. This is imperative for group success.

> *"Don't judge each day by the harvest you reap, but by the seeds you plant."*
>
> —Robert Louis Stevenson

Discussion from Previous Week

The previous week was spent creating a mission statement In review:

- Describe the two projects chosen from the assignment. What were the results of your efforts?

- Was there any facet of the week where you made a decision based on the alignment with the agreed-upon mission statement? Share that situation and how you might have chosen another option had there not been a filtering of logic through the mission statement.

- How has this group philosophy shifted the way you are thinking about your leadership efforts now and in the future? Has it opened your perspective to see a bigger picture?

- Finally, recall the Line Game and express how the exercise influenced your thoughts about leadership. How are they applicable to the leadership journey ahead?

- An overall view of the week:

  1. What was the benefit of your investment to time, effort, energy?
  2. What kind of impact do you think you had on others?
  3. What was the reaction of those around you to your servitude leadership contribution?

Goal Setting: The Blueprint For All To Follow

The previously created mission statement is the foundation of goal setting. Creative goal setting is the process of putting together a blueprint of PRAGMATIC, MEASURABLE benchmarks designed to support forward progress for the group.

Goal setting is a fun exercise, but it often goes no further than the final template. If you are to lead, you must be able to identify what works, what doesn't work, make the necessary adjustments, and continue on the path to reach the destination.

While you certainly want a positive philosophical theme, it is important to designate parameters to support the various goals. Such platitudes as *work harder, do better, include everyone,* etc., are all well and good, but it is important to identify ways of measuring them. *How* do you work harder? *What* determines if you do better? *How* will you include everyone? It is important to define the goals so they can be quantified and measured.

Seek ways to advance the organization from where it is to where it can be. It is tempting to get caught in the comfort zone of *we've always done it this way.* Traditions are a wonderful part of every group's history, but if the tradition is hampering future growth, you must be willing to take a bold step forward and honor the mission statement by making the necessary changes.

Creative goals indicate they are:

- different
- new
- contemporary
- wanted and needed for the welfare of all concerned
- creative
- realistic
- relative

Case Study
> *"We certainly won't arrive if we don't know our destination."*

This quote is the very reason we have goals in the first place. With that said, however, putting together an outline of goals does not guarantee end-all success. There is much work to do from intention to outcome, and the commitment and dedication needed to arrive is where true leadership comes into play.

Chapter 4 Overview
Communication: Part 1

Communication is always the answer to fueling forward momentum as well as resolving any kind of group conflict. Communication is a skill that improves with ongoing practice. It is the key to efficient and effective leadership.

"What we hope ever to do with ease we must learn first to do with diligence."

—Samuel Johnson
(1709–1784) British author

Discussion from Previous Week

Each person was assigned 4 pragmatic/measurable creative goals, promoting the mission statement, to have completed by our next meeting.

- How much were you able to accomplish? Be very truthful!
- On a scale of 1 to 10, how effective do you think you were?
- What was the reaction of those around you? Did you get any feedback from people? If so, what was it?
- What was the leadership benefit you derived from the experience?
- Do you think you made a difference? Why or why not?

The Essence of All Leadership Success: Communication

It has been said,
"All problems can be solved with communication,
and all problems stem from lack of communication."

Communication is the fuel for all leadership. We tend to think communication is about giving instructions, or delegating, or passing out information, etc. Nothing could be further from the truth.

Noted author Robert Bolton ("People Skills") offers this important data concerning communication:

- VERBAL COMMUNICATION: 10% retention (out of 100%).
  He claims: In verbal communication there is far more to it than the shared words: 7% is the word itself, 38% of the interpretation is assigned to the TONE of the voice as the words are spoken, and 55% of the message is translated in the body language of the person who is sharing the words.

- VISUAL COMMUNICATION: 24% retention (out of 100%).
  When the message is extended with the visual support, there is an increase in the staying power of the communication. We often "hear with our eyes." This emphasizes the importance of eye-contact with our colleagues in all communication exchanges.

- TACTILE/KINESTHETIC/PHYSICAL MOVEMENT
  COMMUNICATION: 80% retention (out of 100%).
  When people are "actively" involved in the communication
  exchange, and they are investing some physical/tactile energy in the
  "conversation," the retention rate jumps dramatically. Thus, it is
  always advantageous to communicate in a fashion that "includes" the
  recipient of the message in some form of activity.

Case Study

In every situation of conflict-resolution, the final outcome is based on
communication. It overrides the assumption that is often the problem in the
first place. Psychologists, psychiatrists, counselors, attorneys, business leaders,
political figures all rely on communication as their platform of exchange.

By definition: Communication is the activity of conveying information
through the exchange of thoughts, messages, or information, as by speech,
visuals, signals, writing, or behavior. Communication is "any act by which one
person gives to or receives from another person information about the person's
needs, desires, perceptions, knowledge, or affective states. Communication may
be intentional or unintentional, may involve conventional or unconventional
signals, may take linguistic or nonlinguistic forms, and may occur through
spoken or other modes."

The Relationship This Has to Leadership

Communication is derived from COMMUNITY:
"with unity."

Communication is designed to bring people together who share a common
goal, cause, and/or mission. It is the leader's #1 tool for success (and/or failure)
in any and all situations.

Communication is a skill, and the more we practice it, the better we
become at sending and receiving. Through everything from enhancing one's
vocabulary to increasing the frequency and quality of outreach, it all comes
back to effective communication.

Chapter 5 Overview
Communication: Part 2

Advanced communication—the real deal. Chapter 5 is an amplification of
the previous assignment. The master communicators/leaders have the ability
to "get behind the eyes" of their followers, and they frame their outreach
communication to have personal relevance to those they are leading.

*"You get the best effort from others not by lighting a fire beneath them,
but by building a fire within."*

—Bob Wilson

Discussion from Previous Week

- Did you fulfill your promises?
- What was accomplished?
- What did not get achieved?

Plan for the next step in completion.

Building trust relationships via communcation: The foundation of all organizational achievement

The absolute needed agreement in all leadership success is built on trust.

"The fundamental basis of ALL effective communication is TRUST!"
We follow people we trust.

Trust is the basis for quality communication. Unless we trust someone, there is always a suspicion we might be at the mercy of some self-serving individual who has a hidden agenda, so we stand back until we are absolutely certain we are on solid ground before contributing our best efforts.

Trust is: an assured reliance on the character, ability, strength, and truthful communication of another.

Case Study
Enjoy this. It is the spirit of trust:

> Little girl and her father were crossing a bridge.
> The father was kind of scared so he asked his little daughter,
> "Sweetheart, please hold my hand so that you don't fall into
> the river."
> The little girl said, "No, Dad. You hold my hand."
> "What's the difference?" asked the puzzled father.
> "There's a big difference," replied the little girl.
> "If I hold your hand and something happens to me,
> chances are that I may let your hand go.

But if you hold my hand, I know for sure that no matter what happens, you will never let my hand go."

—Author unknown

In any relationship, the essence of trust is not in its bind, but in its bond. So hold the hand of the followers who love you rather than expecting them to hold yours.

Since you are asking your colleagues to follow your lead, they must know they have your support from the onset. The ultimate outcome of any great leader is to have his or her followers fly on their own...best described in this short bit of wisdom from French poet Apollinaire Guillaume:

> "Come to the edge," he said.
> They said, "We are afraid."
> "Come to the edge," he said.
> They came. He pushed them...and they flew.

The Relationship This Has to Leadership

A true leader understands the difference between KNOWLEDGE and WISDOM. Knowledge (information) can be accumulated at warp speed; however, unless the knowledge is translated and applied to the situation at hand, it is just mere knowledge. By building a trusting relationship with each and every follower, the information then can become wisdom as it is used in a pragmatic fashion to serve everyone in the group.

This is clearly based on the leadership ability to communicate the *why* aspect of the given challenge. It is one thing to tell people *what* to do, and another to explain *how* to do it, but unless the follower knows *why* (the reason for the leader's request), then the full potential (synergy) of the group will never be reached.

Every good leader will first communicate the why, then the how, and finally the what. To achieve this end, there has to be sense of trust fueling the exchange.

Chapter 6 Overview

Building Trust Relationships

"We follow those we trust." Creating and nurturing the ongoing trust relationships is *the key* to developing loyal support. Leaders cannot assume the members of the group will follow in a lock-step manner. Trust is earned and supported via personal communication. Consider the relationship of Chapters 4, 5, and 6.

"Appreciative words are the most powerful force for good on earth!"

—George W. Crane

Discussion from Previous Week

The prior week's theme, "communication as it relates to trust," was dedicated to seeing a situation from behind the eyes of others. Instead of looking at it through your own perspective, make an effort to see the situation from a new viewpoint; thus, offering a better avenue of communication by having the ability to "see both sides."

- What was discovered via your outreach communication?

- How did this shift the communication and ultimately the relationship with this new person?

- What was the advantage of "choosing to understand before being understood"?

- Do you feel this recalibrating of your viewpoint makes a difference in the communication?

- Was it a valuable investment of time, effort, energy?

- Did it help fuel things in a more positive, productive fashion that you can transfer to all of your relationships?

- What worthy addition did it bring to your leadership toolbox?

- How can you use this understanding to benefit future leadership challenges?

Creating a Win-Win Outcome for All

We/Us over I/Me

As you can see, Lesson #6 is a continuation of the *Communication* theme. Since it clearly is the most important skill of the successful leader, let's explore the next level of communication "through the eyes of a servant leader."

Society tends to live from a posture of I/Me.
WIIFM: "What's in it for me?"

If this is the basis of all decision/choice-making, we are doomed to keep all of our energy/potential focused on a self-serving agenda. We/Us thinking allows the leader to open the flanks of creative thinking and discover ways to contribute to all those who choose to be followers.

Case Study

"We harvest what we plant."

To achieve a We/Us posture requires the ability to delay gratification. It is an outgrowth of the GIVING theme. Enjoy this short story:

What Goes Around Comes Around
—author unknown

One day a man saw an old lady stranded on the side of the road, but even in the dim light of day he could see she needed help. So he pulled up in front of her Mercedes and got out. His Pontiac was still sputtering when he approached her.

Even with the smile on his face, she was worried. No one had stopped to help for the last hour or so. Was he going to hurt her? He didn't look safe; he looked poor and hungry. He could see that she was frightened, standing out there in the cold. He knew how she felt. It was those chills that only fear can put in you. He said, "I'm here to help you, ma'am. Why don't you wait in the car where it's warm? By the way, my name is Bryan Anderson."

Well, all she had was a flat tire, but for an old lady, that was bad enough. Bryan crawled under the car looking for a place to put the jack, skinning his knuckles a time or two. Soon he was able to change the tire, but he had to get dirty and his hands hurt.

As he was tightening up the lug nuts, she rolled down the window and began to talk to him. She told him that she was from St. Louis and was only just passing through. She couldn't thank him enough for coming to her aid.

Bryan just smiled as he closed her trunk. The lady asked how much she owed him. Any amount would have been all right with her. She already imagined all the awful things that could have happened had he not stopped. Bryan never thought twice about being paid. This was not a job to him. This was helping someone in need, and heaven knows there were plenty who had given him a hand in the past. He had lived his whole life that way, and it never occurred to him to act any other way. He told her that if she really wanted to pay him back, the next time she saw someone who needed help she could give that person the assistance they needed, and Bryan added, "And think of me." He waited until she started her car and drove off. It had been a cold and depressing day, but he felt good as he headed for home, disappearing into the twilight.

A few miles down the road, the lady saw a small cafe. She went in to grab a bite to eat and take the chill off before she made the last leg of her trip home. It was a dingy-looking restaurant. Outside were two old gas pumps. The whole scene was unfamiliar to her. The waitress came over and brought a clean towel to wipe her wet hair. She had a sweet smile, one that even being on her feet for the whole day couldn't erase. The lady noticed the waitress was nearly eight months pregnant, but she never let the strain and aches change her attitude. The old lady wondered how someone who had so little could be so giving to a stranger. Then she remembered Bryan.

After the lady finished her meal, she paid with a $100 bill. The waitress quickly went to get change for her $100 bill, but the old lady had slipped right out the door. She was gone by the time the waitress came back. The waitress wondered where the lady could be. Then she noticed something written on the napkin.

There were tears in her eyes when she read what the lady wrote: "You don't owe me anything. I have been there, too. Somebody once helped me out, the way I'm helping you. If you really want to pay me back, here is what you do: Do not let this chain of love end with you." Under the napkin were four more $100 bills.

Well, there were tables to clear, sugar bowls to fill, and people to serve, but the waitress made it through another day. That night when she got home from work and climbed into bed, she was thinking about the money and what the lady had written. How could the lady have known how much she and her husband needed it? With the baby due next month, it was going to be hard. She knew how worried her husband was, and as he lay sleeping next to her, she gave him a soft kiss and whispered soft and low, "Everything's going to be all right. I love you, Bryan Anderson."

There is an old saying: "What goes around comes around."

Chapter 7 Overview
Random Acts of Kindness

Going above and beyond the call of duty is the mark of a first-class leader. It's far more than merely meeting standards. Rather, it offers the chance to bring unexpected benefits to those who have chosen to be a part of the organization.

"Blessed are those who can give without remembering and take without forgetting."

—Elizabeth Bibesco

Discussion from Previous Week

The assignment from the last meeting (which included a conversation without using the words *I, me,* and *my*; along with the anonymous note of appreciation; and, finally, befriending someone who you see needs special attention) is a giant step forward. The shift of attention (to the follower) is the basis for all servitude leadership. Congratulations!

- What was the reaction to any or all of the above investments? Were you surprised by the response you received (or didn't receive)?

- How did you feel about your leadership potential following the various exercises?

- Did it avail you to other thoughts/possibilities of how you could continue to develop your leadership skills with others? If so, share these new awarenesses.

Going Above and Beyond the Requisite Assignment

It is important to distinguish between *managers* and **leaders.** Managers do *things right*; leaders do *right things*. Leaders take the initiative; they are always on alert about advancing the mission for the benefit of all. Simply put: Look around and **see what needs to be done**.

Assignment

Random acts of kindness are, for the most part, a quiet contribution to the welfare of another person who is often ignored or taken for granted, and while others are the benefactors of the person's contribution, it is rarely acknowledged and seldom celebrated.

Example:

The school secretary is always available to greet guests, answer any and all questions, serve as the directional guidepost for anyone who needs information, be in charge of all aspects of the systemic welfare of the faculty and student body. Has anyone taken the time to deliver a handwritten note of thanks and a decorated cupcake to this very important person? The same template is true for all members of the school's staff, faculty, administrators, community leaders, etc.

Perhaps there is someone who isolates himself or herself in the cafeteria; here is an opportunity to politely ask to join the person and discover more about him or her. It is the chance to involve the individual in a conversation with the emphasis spotlight on him or her, and to exercise the learned communication skills to build a newfound level of trust.

Complete the following steps to create random acts of kindness:

1. Identify 3 things you feel would be a valuable contribution to the purposeful mission of the group framed as random acts of kindness.

2. Rank them in priority order.

Case Study
Teacher: Use one of your own stories here.

It's grand to be the receiver of a random act of kindness, but it is even greater to be the source of one.

Case Study #1

Several years ago while teaching a class at the local university, during the semester I happened to mention (in passing) that I was a big fan of Oscar Peterson (the famous jazz pianist). At the conclusion of the semester, several of the students passed along very kind notes, special cards, and some delightful gifts. One of the young ladies waited until everyone had left the room, then walked forward and said, "I have truly enjoyed this class, and have learned so much. In return for all your efforts I wanted to offer my appreciation by giving you something I think you will enjoy." She handed me a packet full of CDs featuring the lifetime works of Oscar Peterson. Certainly the gift itself was grand, but the fact that she spent endless hours gathering the recordings and consolidating them into one source was priceless.

Case Study #2:

A dear friend is a fan of a specific kind of potato chip produced by a small family-owned business in a remote part of the country. I was traveling near the location, and although time was short (isn't it always?), I made the decision to extend the trip to stock up on some of those "favorite chips" for my friend. When the gift was delivered, it was one of the most gratifying and memorable moments of my life. He was thrilled...he loved the potato chips, but the real gift was the random act of kindness. It served as a grand reminder to always be "thinking of others" and finding various ways to embellish their lives.

The Relationship This Has to Leadership

We are worth what we give away.

Servitude leadership is based on giving, and there are countless possibilities surrounding us each and every day. Ironically, this is the manifestation of all of the leadership lessons to date, for it creates a win-win outcome for everyone involved.

Leadership is FOR GIVING.

Chapter 8 Overview
Standing in Their Shoes

"Choose to understand before being understood." The truly insightful leaders have the ability to see the landscape ahead by looking at all the perspectives offered by those who are part of the group. This emphasizes an understanding of *we/us* and promotes collective alignment.

> *"Not the maker of plans and promises, but rather the one who offers faithful service in small matters. This is the person who is most likely to achieve what is good and lasting."*

—Johann Wolfgang Von Goethe
(1749–1832)
German poet, dramatist, novelist

Discussion from Previous Week

Week #7 focused on random acts of kindness. This is a major step forward in the entire student leadership curriculum, for it requires action taken that may or may not have an immediate impact on the receiver of the initiative. It is imperative to be totally honest about the follow-through of the planned Random Act of Kindness.

- Did you actually fulfill the self-assigned Random Act of Kindness.

- What was the reaction of those who were the recipients of the Random Act of Kindness, if any?

- Did you receive any feedback from them that you either expected or didn't expect? What was it?

- What would you do different in the execution of your next Random Act of Kindness?

- Did you make a difference in the lives of others through this endeavor? If so, what do you think was the outcome of your investment of effort and energy?

Seeking to Understand from Behind the Eyes of Followers

> The common traits that we find in all great leaders:
> The wherewithal to **stand in their shoes**,
> **to see** from behind **the eyes of others**,
> to **pro-act** for **the welfare of all**
> **instead of react** to the I/Me agenda of the day,
> **choosing to understand before being understood.**

This week's theme highlights one of the most important aspects of the leadership pathway.
Simply put:
It is viewing every situation through a We/Us filter as opposed to the typical "What's in it for me?" viewpoint. When we can make decisions/choices and enlist the energy of any and/or all of the followers, then we have created synergy, the interaction of multiple elements in a system to produce an effect different from or greater than the sum of their individual effects.
Synergy is accomplished through:
- Inclusion of others
- Empowering the followers

It is the key to creating organizational success at the highest level.

Creating a win-win scenario requires one to be able to set aside the ego and stand back to see what is best for all. It is one of the most difficult yet important aspects of a servant leader. While it may seem that you are giving up power, it is (ironically) the ultimate power when the emphasis is on the welfare of the group rather than the satisfaction of personal wants.

The Relationship This Has to Leadership

Effective leadership is based (in part) on supporting the goals of the followers. When we have the ability to understand the posture of others, it affords a great opportunity to make leadership choices that will benefit them and, in turn, uplift the entire organization, thus bringing success to the leader in the process. The leader's ultimate goal is to support the ongoing positive growth and development of the followers.

Chapter 9 Overview
Going the Extra Mile

Chapter 9 highlights the importance of doing more than needs to be done. It is about putting an extra degree of attention on each and every aspect of the leadership agenda. Going the extra mile means exceeding the expectations of all those who are impacted by the leader's work ethic.

"Only those who will risk going too far can possibly find out how far they can go."

—T. S. Eliot

Discussion from Previous Week

People, for the most part, do not like to deal with confrontation. In fact, they will avoid it, deny it, and do everything possible to keep from facing some of the less-than-favorable issues that caused the distancing in the first place. Make a personal commitment to embrace all challenges.

- Were there any breakthroughs as a result of "extending an 1"?

- What did you discover about yourself in the process?

- How do you see this being relevant to your present and future leadership skills?
- Will this impact the way you handle various situations in the future? How?

Making a Differenece by Taking the Initiative
Go the extra mile.

- Try harder to please someone or to get the task done correctly. Try to do more than you are required to do to reach a goal.

- "I like **working with** this particular person because they always **go the extra mile**."

- Help others do more than is expected.

The difference between good and great has much to do with *going the extra mile*. Most people will meet the minimum, but it is the rare few who will take the time to go above and beyond the given expectations.

Chapter 10 Overview

Developing and Maintaining a Positive Attitude:

Becoming the Ultimate Role Model

"We can't lead others until we lead ourselves." Self-improvement is not merely something one does, but it is something one *is*. Ultimately, the admired leader is the person who "walks the talk" with a sense of purpose recognized by all.

"Before you can inspire with emotion, you must be swamped with it yourself.
Before you can move their tears, your own must flow.
To convince them,
you must yourself believe."

—Winston Churchill
(1874–1965)
British statesman, Prime Minister

Discussion from Previous Week
Last week's template of the *"What If?"* exercise offered a to-do list for all leaders.
    We created the *vision* and made the *commitment* to the goal. Now, did you take action? Achieve the goal? Achieve a segment of the goal?

- Did you notice any difference in the followers based on the "going the extra mile" effort? What was it?
- Based on your completion (or incompletion) of your action, how do you see this becoming a cornerstone of all your future leadership actions?

Demonstrating Exemplary Leadership by "Walking the Talk"

The term *attitude* has many connotations.

By definition it means "an expression of favor or disfavor toward a person, place, thing, or event."

Prominent psychologist Gordon Allport once described attitude as "the most distinctive and indispensable concept in contemporary social psychology."

Based on the assumption that "we can't lead others until we lead ourselves," the importance of keeping oneself in the best of spirits is one of the most important main drives of the leadership tapestry. It is best described in the popular quote from noted author Charles Swindoll:

> "The longer I live, the more I realize the impact of attitude on life. Attitude, to me, is more important than facts, it is more important than the past, the education, the money, the circumstances, than failure, than successes, than what other people think or say or do. It is more important than appearance, giftedness, or skill. It will make or break a company...a church...a home. The remarkable thing is, we have a choice every day regarding the attitude we will embrace for that day. We cannot change our past, we cannot change the fact that people will act in a certain way. We cannot change the inevitable. The one thing we can do is play on the one string we have, and that is our attitude. I am convinced that life is 10% what happens to me and 90% of how I react to it. And so it is with you...we are in charge of our attitudes."

Everyone wants to be successful. Even those who say they don't want to be successful have chosen that goal because of the fear of success. We also are aware the driving force behind our personal motivation is wrapped with our attitude; and it, in fact, can determine our future.

In the words of Henry Ford:

"Whether we think we can or whether we think we can't, we are always right."

With that in mind, we know how important it is to control our self-talk, our thoughts, which, in turn, determine our attitude.

- Watch your thoughts; they become your words.
- Watch your words; they become your actions.
- Watch your actions; they become your habits.

- Watch your habits; they become your character.
- Watch your character; it becomes your destiny.

While the human is a member of the animal family, one of the greatest distinctions comes from the fact that we can choose our behavior, we can choose our pathway, we can choose our attitudes. This could well be the most important choice you will ever make in your life!

Chapter 11 Overview

Advancement of the Group by Focusing on Cooperation Over Competition

"When the tide goes up, all boats rise." There is always a desire for "betterment," but not at the expense of others. Synergy is derived at the highest level when the finish line creates a win-win scenario for everyone.

> *"If your actions inspire others to dream more, learn more,*
> *do more, and become more, you are a leader."*
>
> —John Quincy Adams

Discussion from Previous Week

The week of building one's own self-worth by building others self-esteem offers the next level of leadership contribution. It is the next step towards leadership inspiration.

- Were there any surprise reactions from your unexpected recognition of someone's value? If so, what were they?

- What was your own feeling following one of the communications? Is it what you thought it would be? Share your thoughts.

- What did you learn from the process and how do you intend to integrate it into your future communications?

- How do you see your attitude impacting your leadership effectiveness?

We Are All In This Together!

As we draw to the end of this student leadership curriculum, the weight of the responsibility increases proportionately: from serving oneself, to recognizing our colleagues, and now taking on the task of care and support of the entire group.

It is the ultimate responsibility of the leader to stay the course while protecting the flock. It is best described by this leadership philosophy:

The captain goes down with the ship.

The idiom literally means that a captain will be the last person to leave a ship alive prior to its sinking or utter destruction, and if unable to evacuate his crew and passengers, the captain will not evacuate himself. In maritime law, the responsibility of the ship's master for his ship is paramount no matter what its condition, so abandoning a ship has legal consequences.

Succeeding in this realm requires the ability to realize the value of cooperation over competition. This does not diminish the importance of competition, but it amplifies the importance of cooperation, and it also reinforces the win-win concept of leadership.

"Being a part of an agenda beyond ourselves liberates us to complement each other rather than compete with each other."

—Joseph Stowell

The Relationship This Has to Leadership

When one understands the power of cooperation, it shifts the paradigm of all decision/choice making:

Cooperation is the process of working or acting together. In its simplest form, it involves things working in harmony; in its more complicated form, it can involve something as complex as the inner workings of a human being or even the social patterns of a nation. It is the opposite of working separately in competition.

Ultimately, group welfare is based on the attitude the leader espouses after each and every get-together. There must be a common support of all if we hope to increase the standards for all.

"When the tide goes up, all boats rise."

ASK YOURSELF
How do you see yourself contributing to this?
How does it relate to you? Your life?

The concept of cooperation to support the entire organization is an amplification of the win-win concept. Instead of reacting negatively when some members of the organization are not pulling their weight, the leader immediately begins to evaluate the situation and seeks various ways to recalibrate the energies to get everyone back on track.

Each day provides countless opportunities to put this knowledge into action…from lending a helping hand, to picking up some extra responsibility for a colleague who is simply in over his or her head.

The leader is (in fact) the go-to person, and the go-to person is the one who can help others complete their tasks, resolve their problems, lighten their load.

Chapter 12 Overview

Not the Final Chapter, But the Beginning of the Leadership Journey

Leadership is a way of being. The last chapter of the leadership study guide serves as a challenge to integrate the various concepts learned throughout the twelve-week curriculum. It is the opportunity to turn knowledge into wisdom for the welfare of those who have chosen to commit personal time, effort, and energy to the defined organization.

"When the best leader's work is done, the people say, 'We did it ourselves.'"

—Lao Tzu

Discussion from Previous Week

- What did you discover that wanted/needed your leadership attention skills? What was the result of your action?

- In what ways do you see this "sensitive outreach" impacting the group, the individual, *you*?

- Did you notice any other avenues where cooperation can generate greater results than competition? Where? How?

The more we know, the more we know we don't know; this is the new beginning!

Materials needed for this lesson:
- Number cards

From intention to outcome:
- manifest your dreams.

As we come to the last chapter of the leadership program, it is apparent you must now create your own leadership program. You must fill in the gap from KNOWLEDGE to EXPERIENCE, and that requires taking the newly discovered understandings and starting the process all over again, but it will mean something far different this time.

Most importantly, notice how you perceive things in a different fashion. Advance yourself from your present leadership status to exceptional leadership:

- Exceptional Leadership

  Learning to utilize or sharpen existing leadership tools, skills, and techniques along your personal and organizational path to achievement.

- Exceptional Conversations

  Ensuring that clean, safe, and effective conversations occur when creating or owning accountability both internally and externally for you and your organization.

- Exceptional Relationships

  Creating, maintaining, and growing relationships with those who work alongside of you and those you lead.

- Exceptional Connections

  Causing and ensuring meaningful connections between you and those you serve.

The Relationship This Has to Leadership

We are reminded, again, that leadership isn't something we *do*, but it is something we *are*. Whatever we *want* is (paradoxically) what we *give away*.

BE REMINDED:

Leadership is not so much about technique and methods as it is about opening the heart. Leadership is about inspiration of oneself and of others. Great leadership is about human experiences, not processes. Leadership is not a formula or a program; it is a human activity that comes from the heart and considers the hearts of others as well. It is an attitude, not a routine.

Servitude leadership is about (literally) serving others. If we cite the great leaders in history, they were often those who were not politically postured but who were dedicated to making the world a better place for all.

Servitude leadership is both a leadership philosophy and a set of leadership practices. Traditional leadership generally involves the accumulation and exercise of power by one at the "top of the pyramid." By comparison, the servitude leader shares power, puts the needs of others first, and helps people develop and perform as highly as possible.

About the Author

Tim Lautzenheiser

Tim Lautzenheiser began his teaching career at Northern Michigan University. He then moved to the University of Missouri and from there to New Mexico State University. During that time, he developed highly acclaimed groups in both instrumental and vocal music.

Following his tenure in the college band directing world, he spent 3 years with McCormick's Enterprises working as Executive Director of Bands of America. In 1981, he founded Attitude Concepts for Today, Inc., an organization designed to manage the many requests for teacher in-service workshops, student leadership seminars, and convention speaking engagements that focus on the area of effective leadership training. After 30-plus years of clinic presentations, some 3 million students have experienced one of his popular sessions.

Tim Lautzenheiser presently serves as Vice President of Education for Conn-Selmer, Inc. He is a nationally recognized voice touting the importance of arts education for every child. His books, published by GIA Publications, Inc., continue to be best-sellers in the educational community. He is also co-author of the popular band method, *Essential Elements*. He is also Senior Educational Consultant for Hal Leonard, Senior Educational Advisor for Music for All and NAMM (the National Association of Music Merchants).

Tim Lautzenheiser holds degrees from Ball State University and the University of Alabama. In 1995, he was awarded an Honorary Doctorate from the VanderCook College of Music. In addition, he is a member of the Midwest Clinic Board of Directors and the Western International Band Clinic/ American Band College Board of Directors.